THE
BIBLE
IN
ONE HOUR

THE
BIBLE
IN
ONE HOUR

Stan Campbell

NEW YORK   BOSTON   NASHVILLE

Compilation copyright © 2016 by Stan Campbell
The Bible in One Hour copyright © 2006 by Stan Campbell
Pocket Bible Trivia copyright © 2007 by Stan Campbell

Cover designed by JuLee Brand
Cover images by ShutterStock
Cover copyright © 2016 by Hachette Book Group, Inc.

FaithWords
Hachette Book Group
1290 Avenue of the Americas, New York, NY 10104
faithwords.com
twitter.com/faithwords

The Bible in One Hour was originally published by Viking Canada in 2006.

The Bible in One Hour was previously published in the U.S. in hardcover as *Bible to Go* by FaithWords in August 2007.

Pocket Bible Trivia was previously published in the U.S. in hardcover as *Bibleology* by FaithWords in September 2007.

First Compilation Edition: November 2016

FaithWords is a division of Hachette Book Group, Inc. The FaithWords name and logo are trademarks of Hachette Book Group, Inc.

The publisher is not responsible for websites (or their content) that are not owned by the publisher.

The Hachette Speakers Bureau provides a wide range of authors for speaking events. To find out more, go to www.hachettespeakersbureau.com or call (866) 376-6591.

Library of Congress Control Number: 2016943216

ISBNs: 978-1-4555-3960-4 (paper over board), 978-1-4555-3961-1 (ebook)

Printed in the United States of America

WOR

10 9 8 7 6 5 4 3 2 1

CONTENTS

INTRODUCTION		vii
ONE	Beginnings	3
TWO	The Patriarchs: From Mesopotamia to Israel	8
THREE	The Wilderness: Out of Egypt and Home Again	16
FOUR	Settling Down: Building a Nation	22
FIVE	Wisdom Literature: Songs, Stories, Sayings, and Sex	30
SIX	Divided and Conquered: The Fall of the Nation and the Rise of the Prophets	37
SEVEN	Back Home: The Return to Jerusalem	44
EIGHT	Jesus: His Humanity	49
NINE	Jesus: His Teachings	56
TEN	Jesus: His Divinity	61
ELEVEN	The Early Church	69
TWELVE	Paul: His Life and Ministry	75
THIRTEEN	Paul: His Letters	80
FOURTEEN	Other New Testament Letters	86
FIFTEEN	Revelation: The Big Finish	92
APPENDIX		97
ABOUT THE AUTHOR		104

Introduction

Countless people have set out to better understand the Bible and have sooner or later come away discouraged...thwarted...frustrated. Certainly the task is a daunting one. Even with the multitude of current translations and paraphrases, the Bible can be difficult to understand. It is thick, occasionally perplexing, and contains no shortage of tongue-twisting names and places.

One common complaint is that the Bible is too ancient. Its events cover a span of 4,000 years or so, and certain portions conjure up dry high school lectures on the Fertile Crescent, Assyria, Babylon, the Greek and Roman empires, and other bygone eras. Knowledge of such topics can be helpful in certain portions of Scripture, but the Bible is so much more than ancient history!

Another common criticism is that it's hard to connect the portions of the Bible that we *do* know. Many people know the basic accounts of Noah, Jonah, Paul, Esther, Samson, Jesus, Abraham, David, and others, but they would be hard-pressed to put the stories in chronological sequence on a time line. In addition, Scripture can seem to be a mélange of history, poetry, prophecy, narrative story, law, and more.

This book is intended to alleviate such problems...in about an hour. Woven throughout the Bible is a story line, a plot. We will follow that flow of action from start to finish, from Genesis to Revelation. We won't be able to go in-depth, of course, but we can cover the high points, connecting the dots of what you already know while providing (brief!) historical context.

Then comes the fun part! Once you see the big picture, you can begin to explore various specific portions of Scripture with more confidence. It will take about an hour to read this book, yet plumbing the depths of Scripture is an adventure that will take the rest of your life. You will quickly discover that the Bible is not an old, outdated, irrelevant book. It is the "living and active" Word of God that continues to speak to people today (see Hebrews 4:12).

I hope the hour you devote to reading this book will be an investment that pays off for years to come. And as you get to know the Bible better, may you also grow closer to its Author.

THE
BIBLE
IN
ONE HOUR

ONE

Beginnings

It's always good to start at the beginning, yet at the beginning of the Bible we find God already present (Genesis 1:1). The theological belief that God is eternal means not only that he will exist forever into the future but also that he has always existed into the eternity of the past.

Creation (GENESIS 1–2)

You'll notice that it's completely dark as we begin our journey through the Bible. We're also in a place that is formless and empty. But all it takes is a word from God and immediately there is light. Another word, and the sky and earth separate. A few more words, and the new world is teeming with plants, animals, and the first human beings (see pages 97–98). After each day of

Creation, God declares his work "good." After human-kind is established, however, God evaluates all he has done and deems it "very good" (Genesis 1:31).

Adam and Eve (GENESIS 2:15–3:24)

Adam, the first created human, is assigned the task of naming all the animals. In doing so, he notices that for him there is "no suitable helper" (Genesis 2:20), so God places him in a deep sleep and uses one of his ribs to create Eve. God places them in the Garden of Eden, naked but without shame.

Eden is a paradise. But in time, Adam and Eve do the one thing God has instructed them not to do. After being tempted by a serpent, they succumb and eat of the fruit of the tree of the knowledge of good and evil. As a result, they recognize their nakedness and hide from God.

This "original sin" initiates a separation from God that has made it more difficult for humans to interact with him throughout the centuries. It results, too, in a curse on the serpent, on Adam (thorns, thistles, and sweat as impediments to future work) and Eve (pain in childbirth and subjection to her husband). But it also results in the Bible's first messianic prophecy: A time will come when a descendant of Adam and Eve (Jesus) will "crush the head" of the serpent (Satan), even though the serpent will "strike his heel" (Genesis 3:14–19).

Cain and Abel (GENESIS 4:1–16)

After Adam and Eve are evicted from Eden (to prevent their eating from the tree of life and living forever in a state of separation from God), it doesn't take long for sin to spread. When God rejects an offering from their older son, Cain, and accepts one from their younger son, Abel, Cain responds in a fit of jealousy. He lures Abel into a field and commits the first premeditated murder. When questioned by God, he tries to plead ignorance—to no avail.

Early Personalities (GENESIS 4:17–5:32)

Soon afterward we come to Lamech, who was the first known polygamist, and boastful as well. But we also read of the first rancher (Jabal), musician (Jubal), and metalworker (Tubal-Cain). And this is where we find the Bible's oldest character: Methuselah, who lives to be 969 years old. With such age spans, it's no surprise that people are fruitful and multiply, and the population grows.

But so does sin. People live and die and generally ignore God. Yet a couple of people stand out as positive examples. One is Enoch, the father of Methuse-

lah. We are told, "Enoch walked with God; then he was
no more, because God took him away" (Genesis 5:24).
This cryptic statement is better explained in Hebrews
11:5, which tells us that because Enoch pleased God,
God didn't require that Enoch face physical death.

Noah (GENESIS 6–9)

Another exception is Noah, who "was a righteous man,
blameless among the people of his time, and he walked
with God" (Genesis 6:9). Sin has finally reached the
point where "the LORD was grieved that he had made
man on the earth, and his heart was filled with pain"
(Genesis 6:6). At this time, God limits human life
spans to 120 years (Genesis 6:3). He also tells Noah to
build a three-deck ark in anticipation of a devastating
flood. The ark is to be 450 feet long, 75 feet wide, and
45 feet high. By the time he finishes it, Noah is 600
years old. Two of every kind of bird and animal come
to him, and he boards them along with seven pairs of
clean (kosher) animals and birds, which can be used
for food and, later, for sacrifices. Then God shuts
the animals and eight people (Noah, his wife, his three
sons, and their wives) in the ark.

The rain begins to fall, and the waters also rise up
from "all the springs of the great deep" (Genesis 7:11).
After 40 days, the earth is covered. It takes time for
the waters to recede, however. Noah and his family are

in the ark for just over a year before a dove indicates the land is dry enough for them to disembark (Genesis 7:11, 8:13–14). It is at this point that God provides the rainbow as a sign of the covenant he makes with Noah to never again destroy the earth with a flood (Genesis 9:11–17).

And although God has given humankind a second chance to eliminate the wickedness that had become so rampant, it doesn't take long for sin to return. Noah plants a vineyard, gets drunk, gets naked, and is observed by one of his sons, who ridicules him. When he discovers his son's insult, he places a curse on that son's descendants (who will become the Canaanites).

The Tower of Babel (GENESIS 11:1–9)

And the next major story we come to is of the Tower of Babel, where a community of people is determined to build a tower into the heavens in order to "make a name for ourselves" (Genesis 11:4) and, ostensibly, to share God's glory. But God "confused their language" (Genesis 11:7), so they can no longer communicate with one another, and they scatter to various parts of the world.

So although we've only just begun our journey through the Bible, it's already filled with action. And from here, the pace just picks up. Next comes the era of the patriarchs.

TWO

The Patriarchs

From Mesopotamia to Israel

So far, the action of the Bible has taken place in the "fertile crescent" of the Middle East. The Garden of Eden was located near the confluence of the Tigris and Euphrates Rivers (Genesis 2:10–14). Noah's ark came to rest on Mount Ararat (Genesis 8:4), believed to be in what is now Turkey. The city of Babylon (in modern Iraq) has already been established and the Tower of Babel was nearby. So when does the action of the Bible shift to the land of Israel? Right now.

Abraham (GENESIS 12–23)

A resident of the Mesopotamian city of Ur is named Abram. One day, when he is 75 years old, Abram receives a call from God to leave his home and go to a land God will show him. This is certainly an un-

precedented and curious occurrence, yet we are told,
"So Abram left" (Genesis 12:4).

He travels with his wife, Sarai, his nephew Lot, his
household, his servants, and his flocks. Abra(ha)m continues to be one of the Bible's preeminent examples of
faith, yet he is not without his faults. Twice when he
feels threatened by foreign powers, he passes off his
wife as his sister, allowing her to be added to other
men's harems. But both times God protects her and
returns her, honor intact, to Abram (Genesis 12:10–20,
20:1–17).

Still, Abram is no coward. When Lot is kidnapped
by a coalition of kings, Abram leads a rescue party to
get him back. And when a major disagreement breaks
out between the servants of Abram and the servants
of Lot, it is Uncle Abe who settles the matter by giving
Lot his choice of land on which to settle. (Lot unwisely
chooses the cities of Sodom and Gomorrah.)

As Abram continues to act in faith, God continues
to add to what he has promised him. God promised to
make Abram's name great, to create from him a great
nation, to give him all the land he could see in every
direction, and to give him descendants as numerous as
the stars in the sky. And as one sign of his covenant
with Abram, God changes Abram's name to Abraham:
"father of many."

The problem is that Abraham doesn't yet have a child, and he and Sarah (whose name is also changed by God) are aging fast. So when Abraham reaches 86 (and Sarah is only 10 years younger), Sarah has him sleep with her servant, Hagar, in order to produce an offspring. The resulting child, Ishmael, creates friction within the household. God also reaffirms that Abraham's child is to come from Sarah.

And sure enough, when Abraham is 100 and Sarah is 90, she gives birth to their son and names him Isaac. Through Isaac, the Jewish nation will come to be . . . and through Ishmael, the Arab people. Abram, whose original name meant "exalted father," does indeed become Abraham, the "father of many," and is now revered by the Christians, Jews, and Muslims.

Sodom and Gomorrah (GENESIS 18–19)

Abraham's nephew Lot has settled in the twin cities of sin: Sodom and Gomorrah. God tells Abraham he is planning to destroy the cities. Abraham barters with God, finally getting God to agree to spare the cities if there are even ten righteous people living there. But there aren't.

When a couple of angels go to warn Lot that God is about to destroy his city, a gang of local men attempt to break into Lot's house and have sex with them (thinking they are merely male visitors). The angels strike the crowd with blindness and tell Lot to have his friends and family leave immediately. But when Lot does so, they think he is joking.

At dawn the angels physically pull Lot, his wife, and their two daughters out of the city to safety, telling them to flee to the mountains and warning them not to look back. But Lot's wife turns to look and instantly becomes a pillar of salt. Not long afterward, Lot's daughters take turns getting him drunk and sleeping with him so they can bear children. From their sons, Moab and Ben-Ammi, arise the Moabites and Ammonites, tribes that will cause the Israelites much trouble throughout their history.

Isaac (GENESIS 21–22, 24, 26)

Perhaps the best-known story of Abraham involves his son Isaac. When Isaac is still young, God tests Abraham, instructing him to offer his son as a sacrifice. Abraham responds "early the next morning." The two go to the top of a mountain where Abraham ties down Isaac, raises a knife, and prepares to plunge it into his son. At the last second, an angel calls out to stop him. A ram caught in the underbrush serves as a sacrifice instead, and Abraham passes his test of faith. In the New Testament we are told that Abraham believed

God could raise Isaac from the dead if that's what it took for God to keep his promise (Hebrews 11:17–19).

Later another great Bible story tells of how Abraham sends a servant to find a godly wife for Isaac. In what is clearly an act of God, the servant brings back Rebekah. In a case of "like father, like son," when Isaac finds himself confronted with a foreign king who is attracted to his wife, he says she is his sister and allows her to go with the king. But when the king happens to look out a window and see Isaac and Rebekah making out, it doesn't take him long to figure out that something is wrong. The situation is resolved peacefully, and eventually Isaac and Rebekah become the parents of twins: Jacob and Esau.

Jacob (GENESIS 25:19–34, 27–33)

Despite being twins, Jacob and Esau couldn't be more opposite. Jacob is described as "a quiet man, staying among the tents." Esau is the pride of his father and "a skillful hunter, a man of the openncountry" (Genesis 25:27)

As the older son, Esau should have the "birthright" —all the blessings and benefits usually granted the oldest male in the family. But depending on how you read the Bible, Jacob is either a selfish and wily con man or a masterful and shrewd businessman. (Even as they came out of the womb, Jacob's hand was grasping Esau's heel.) Jacob first catches Esau at a vulnerable moment and gets him to agree to give up his birthright. And later, when Isaac is about to bestow the formal blessing on his older son, Jacob and Rebekah put together an elaborate scheme that completely deceives the twins' blind father, leaving Jacob with the blessing. As a result, he has to leave home to escape Esau's rage.

In his 20 years away, Jacob has a prophetic dream of a staircase into heaven, takes two wives, has eleven sons and a daughter, and accumulates great herds of animals while working for Rebekah's brother, Laban. As he is preparing to return home and confront Esau, he spends a night wrestling with a stranger who turns out to be God. At that point, God changes Jacob's name to Israel (meaning "he struggles with God"). And Jacob's sons become, essentially, the twelve tribes of Israel, or collectively, the Israelites.

After 20 years, Esau forgives Jacob and the two reconcile peacefully.

Joseph (GENESIS 37, 39–50)

Of all his sons, Jacob's favorite by far is Joseph—for many years the only child of Rachel, his true love. A rivalry develops between Joseph and his ten older brothers that becomes so bad that they decide to kill him. But when a caravan comes through, they opt to sell Joseph into slavery instead. To cover their act, they take the fancy coat their father had given Joseph, dip it in goat's blood, and tell Jacob that a wild animal has killed Joseph.

Joseph matures quickly after he is taken to Egypt. He is a faithful servant, both to God and his master, Potiphar, yet Potiphar's wife falsely accuses him of attempted rape and gets him thrown into prison. Even in jail, Joseph's continued faithfulness is rewarded, as he is quickly promoted to oversee the other inmates, leaving the warden with nothing to worry about.

On his eventual release, Joseph interprets a dream for Pharaoh and foresees a 7-year abundant harvest followed by a 7-year drought and famine. Thanks to Joseph, Egypt stocks up on grain, is prepared during the years of famine, and even has enough food stored to supply the surrounding countries. In addition, Joseph is promoted to second in command over the country, subject only to Pharaoh himself.

As an added twist, when the famine hits Israel, Jacob sends his sons to Egypt to buy grain. And there, standing before Joseph and begging for food, are his ten brothers. They don't recognize him, but he knows *them*. He creates a number of situations to see if they have changed, and indeed, they are feeling remorse for their past actions and are emphatically protective of their new "little brother," Benjamin. Eventually, Joseph reveals his identity and extends his forgiveness, assuring them that it was God's plan all along.

Jacob, of course, is overjoyed to discover that Joseph is still alive. And the Egyptian Pharaoh even insists that Joseph's family move to Egypt and live in "the best part of the land"—the region of Goshen (Genesis 47:6).

The book of Genesis concludes with the deaths of Jacob (Israel) and Joseph. But before his death, Joseph makes his brothers swear an oath that when they leave Egypt they will carry his bones with them. It seems a strange request, but as we're about to see, maybe Joseph knew something they didn't.

THREE

The Wilderness
Out of Egypt and Home Again

As our journey through the Bible continues, we will stay in Egypt and let about 400 years pass. During that time, the Israelite presence continues to grow. The seventy people from Joseph's family who migrated to Goshen become a formidable force of hundreds of thousands. Meanwhile, the Egyptian leaders forget about Joseph and his God-given wisdom that allowed Egypt to prosper during a horrible widespread famine.

Moses: His Birth, His Felony, and the Burning Bush (EXODUS 1–3)

As a result, the new Pharaoh has decided to enslave the Israelites. And to make things worse, a command has gone out to kill all male Hebrew babies by throwing them into the Nile River. It is under this death sentence that Moses is born.

But rather than obey the edict, Moses' mother coats a basket with pitch, places it among the reeds of the Nile, and has his big sister watch to see what will happen. The baby cries just as Pharaoh's daughter is taking her bath, and she adopts him, even hiring his own mother to be his wet nurse.

Moses grows up Egyptian, but he is aware of his Hebrew roots. One day, upon witnessing an Egyptian beating a Hebrew, he kills the Egyptian while no one is looking—or so he thinks. But when he discovers that people know what he has done, he flees into the wilderness to escape Pharaoh's wrath. There he marries Zipporah, one of seven daughters of a man named Jethro, and works as a shepherd for his father-in-law.

While out with the sheep one day, Moses comes upon a bush that appears to be burning yet does not burn up. God addresses him by name from the bush and tells him to go lead his people out of Egypt "into a good and spacious land, a land flowing with milk and honey" (Exodus 3:8). Moses is reluctant and offers a number of excuses, but he eventually obeys.

Pharaoh, the Plagues, the Exodus, and the Red Sea (EXODUS 4–14)

Moses returns to Pharaoh and tells him to "let my people go," just as God has instructed, but Pharaoh only intensifies the workload of the Israelites. God then sends a series of plagues upon Egypt—frogs, locusts, hail, darkness, and more. Pharaoh resists plague after plague, even though his country is in turmoil while the land where the Israelites live is spared. But in a final plague, God strikes down the firstborn in all human and livestock families. The Israelites have prepared ahead of time by placing lamb's blood on their doorposts, causing God to pass over their houses with no harm (and instituting the Jewish celebration of Passover). But the deaths in the Egyptian homes are finally what convince Pharaoh to relent and let the Israelites leave.

However, Moses and his people don't get far when Pharaoh changes his mind. The Israelites are camped at the Red Sea as the Egyptian army rides up. The Israelites seem to be trapped, but God instructs Moses to hold his staff over the water, and as he does, the waters part. The Israelites cross on dry ground. As the Egyptians try to follow, their chariot wheels come off and they realize that "the LORD is fighting . . . against Egypt!" (Exodus 14:25). But too late. The waters come down and there are no Egyptian survivors.

Forty Years in the Wilderness

(EXODUS 15–40, LEVITICUS, NUMBERS, DEUTERONOMY)

The presence of God goes before the people in a pillar of cloud by day and a pillar of fire by night. He leads them in a somewhat circuitous route to minimize encounters with threatening nations. He provides fresh water, even from polluted pools and solid rock. He causes manna, which tastes "like wafers made with honey," to fall every day (except the Sabbath) (Exodus 16:31).

Along the way, God has the people stop at Sinai, where he calls Moses to the top of the mountain and gives him laws for the people to live by, including the Ten Commandments (see page 98). God also provides specific plans for the construction of a tabernacle, a portable house of worship for the people during their travels (and precursor to the temple).

But in spite of everything God is doing for them, the people perpetually complain. They don't like the monotony of manna. They fear they will run out of food and water, and that enemies will overpower them. They keep wanting—sometimes demanding—to return to Egypt, where at least they knew what was in store for them (although that meant slavery)!

Even at the edge of the promised land, their final destination, they balk. Twelve spies are sent to scout out the land. It is truly a wonderful place, but the natives are large and intimidating. Ten of the spies recommend turning around and going back. Only two—Joshua and Caleb—insist on entering, and those two are almost stoned by the crowd.

But God has had enough. He is ready to strike the people down with a plague and start over, but Moses intercedes. So instead, God decrees that they must wander in the wilderness for 40 years until the unbelieving generation has died off and is replaced by more faithful people. Upon hearing the news, the remorseful Israelites *then* try to enter the land and are severely routed (Numbers 13–14).

And sure enough, 40 years later the new generation of Israelites is ready to move forward. Moses has been forbidden to enter the promised land because of a frustration-inspired act of disobedience, but God takes him onto a mountain and allows him to see the land before he dies. So it is Joshua who eventually takes the people into the land.

Here are a few important stories from this section of the Bible:

- The bones of Joseph travel with the Israelites (Exodus 13:17–19)
- The golden calf (Exodus 32)
- Moses' sin (Numbers 20:1–13; Deuteronomy 34)
- Balaam and his talking donkey (Numbers 22)
- The Ten Commandments (Exodus 20:3–17; Deuteronomy 5:7–21)
- Rahab and the Israelite spies (Joshua 2)
- A miraculous entry into the promised land (Joshua 3)

• Achan: The effects of one person's sin on a nation
  (Joshua 7)

Joshua and the Promised Land (BOOK OF JOSHUA)

Joshua is an exemplary leader, personally chosen by God to complete the Israelites' journey. The mighty city of Jericho is the first obstacle they face in the new land, but Joshua follows God's instructions to the letter and the walls come tumbling down.

After eliminating the major strongholds, the Israelites divide into tribes and go to their respective areas that God has assigned to them. Their assignment is to completely clear out the natives of the area and establish themselves. They are to show no mercy and to have no interaction with the non-Israelite peoples.

The Israelites are strong and God is with them, yet very few of the tribes do as they have been instructed. If they rid the new land of potential oppressors, they can live in peace and prosperity for a long while. But they don't. And in the next chapter we'll see what happens as a result.

FOUR

Settling Down
Building a Nation

So far in our rapid journey through the Bible, the action has moved from Mesopotamia to Israel, to Egypt, and back to Israel again (the promised land). It is here that the action will take place for a while. Sadly, the people will eventually be forced to leave, but for the next few centuries they will be settling in.

The Judges

The "judges" of this biblical era are by no means what we imagine when we think of courtrooms, flowing robes, and rules of order. The biblical judges are warrior leaders of the nation, called by God to confront powerful enemies during a rough and barbaric time. After the people have settled in the promised land, it doesn't take long for the spiritual commitment of

Israel to decline and then disappear altogether. The motto of this era is well described in the final verse of the book of Judges: "In those days Israel had no king; everyone did as he saw fit" (Judges 21:25).

The book of Judges describes a repeated cycle: (1) people forget about God, (2) God allows various enemies to conquer and rule the Israelites, (3) the Israelites repent and cry out to God for help, (4) God calls a judge to confront and defeat Israel's enemies, and (5) the nation has a lengthy time of peace and freedom. And each time, the people again forget about God, starting yet another cycle.

Of the thirteen or so judges who rule, the better-known ones are Deborah, Gideon, and Samson.

Deborah (JUDGES 4–5)

The judge of this era should be a man named Barak, but he is a hesitant leader. Deborah is a prophetess who tells Barak what he should do, but his reluctance to respond results in Deborah's taking the lead. In addition to Deborah and her leadership, another woman helps end Israel's oppression. Although Deborah and Barak have already routed the enemy, the opposing leader has escaped and is hiding in the tent of a friend. But the wife of that friend, a woman named Jael, puts the evil leader to sleep and then drives a tent peg through his head.

Gideon (JUDGES 6–8)

Gideon is definitely not the world's most dynamic leader. When we first see him, he is threshing wheat in a winepress to avoid being seen by the vicious Midianites, who would most certainly help themselves to his grain. Nevertheless, an angel suddenly appears and says: "The LORD is with you, mighty warrior" (Judges 6:12).

Gideon does everything God asks of him, even when he doesn't seem to have a lot of confidence in himself. He is the one who asks for a sign from God by placing a wool fleece on the ground and asking that in the morning the fleece be wet with dew while the ground be completely dry. And when God does as Gideon asks, Gideon asks for the reverse to occur. The next morning the ground is covered with dew, but the fleece is dry.

God wants to show Gideon what he, God, can do. Gideon has an army of thirty-two thousand soldiers, but God tells him to send home everyone who is scared. Immediately, 22,000 men leave. Then God reduces the remaining 10,000 to only 300. And even then, by following God's instructions, the 300 Israelites defeat the entire Midianite army using torches, pitchers, and trumpets rather than swords. A God-initiated panic causes the Midianites to turn on one another and flee. Thanks to Gideon, the Israelites experience peace for 40 years.

Samson (JUDGES 13–16)

Samson is Gideon's opposite. At God's instructions, Samson's parents raise him as a Nazirite, which means in part that he will never drink wine, eat grape products, or get a haircut (Numbers 6:1–21). Other biblical Nazirites were Samuel (1 Samuel 1:11) and John the Baptist (Luke 1:15).

God has given Samson extraordinary strength, which Samson takes for granted. He disregards his parents' wishes, goes where he wants, gets into fights, and is a sore loser when outsmarted. Even so, God uses Samson to retaliate against the Philistines, who are oppressing Israel at the time. Samson sleeps with their women, single-handedly kills a thousand of their men in a skirmish, removes and carries away their city gates, and escapes every time they try to trap him.

So the Philistines use Samson's self-interest against him. Samson falls in love with a Philistine woman named Delilah, whom the other Philistines hire to find the secret of his strength. He holds out for a while, but eventually he lets her know that his strength is connected to his long hair. When he awakes from a nap, he discovers he is bound and has had a haircut. For the first time in his life, he is helpless.

The Philistines blind Samson and force him to work for them. But when his hair grows back out, his strength returns. At a large religious gathering where the Philistines are making fun of Samson, he pulls down the central pillars of their temple, killing thousands of Philistines and dying in the process.

King Saul (1 SAMUEL 8–31)

After the era of the judges, a prophet-judge named Samuel becomes God's choice of leader. But by this time, the people are demanding a king because "then we will be like all the other nations" (1 Samuel 8:20). The Law that was handed down from Moses has provided for a human king (Deuteronomy 17:14–20), although God is supposed to be Israel's king. But God tells Samuel to do as the people have asked.

The first king is Saul, described as "an impressive young man without equal among the Israelites—a head taller than any of the others" (1 Samuel 9:2). The Philistines are still around and are a constant threat to Israel. Saul has some early military victories, and so does his courageous son Jonathan. But Saul's faith seems to wane in his later years, and he isn't as obedient as he should be. So God begins to prepare another king "after his own heart" (1 Samuel 13:14) to replace Saul.

Saul even consults a witch (medium) for advice, and soon afterward he kills himself after being wounded in a lost battle.

David (I SAMUEL 16–2; SAMUEL 24)

David is God's choice to replace Saul, but the switch isn't quick or easy. First David makes a name for himself by killing the giant Goliath and then winning a number of battles against the Philistines. Saul's jealousy intensifies to the point where he repeatedly tries to kill David. But David refuses to fight back, even though he twice has an ideal opportunity to kill Saul.

After Saul's death, David unites the tribes of Israel and establishes Jerusalem as the capital of the combined kingdom. David seems to do everything right, until later in life when he sees Bathsheba taking a bath, sends for her, and sleeps with her. When she conceives a child while her husband is away at battle, David arranges to have her husband killed. God sends a prophet to confront David, and the child of the affair dies.

In addition, David's life is never again the same. One of his sons (Amnon) rapes his half sister, and another son (Absalom) kills Amnon. In time, Absalom even tries to take over the kingdom from David and dies as a result.

But David repents of his sin. Many of the Psalms are attributed to him, and Psalm 51 is a stark and humble confession of his affair with Bathsheba. Later, David and Bathsheba have another son, Solomon, who will become the next king.

Solomon (1 KINGS 1–11)

David has united the kingdom and conquered Israel's enemies. Solomon begins his reign with peace and quickly establishes a period of prosperity unlike any other in Israel's history. Early on, God offers to give Solomon anything he asks for. Because Solomon asks for wisdom to lead his people, rather than for riches or honor, God gives him wisdom *and* riches *and* honor.

Solomon's great wisdom quickly becomes evident in everything from lawsuits between prostitutes vying for child custody to visits from the queen of Sheba. He writes thousands of proverbs and songs. People come from all over the world just to listen to him. And the wealth of Israel reaches the point where "the king made silver as common in Jerusalem as stones" (1 Kings 10:27). Under Solomon's rule, the boundaries of Israel extend farther than ever before, or since.

Solomon's most significant accomplishment is the building of the temple in Jerusalem. It is a magnificent building dedicated to God. Following the design of the tabernacle, it has a Holy Place, where only priests can enter, and a Most Holy Place, where only the high priest can go and then only once a year, on the Day of Atonement, in order to offer a sacrifice for the sins of the nation.

But in later life Solomon turns to idolatry. He has married 700 wives and also has 300 concubines. Because of his devotion to his wives and their gods, " his heart was not fully devoted to the LORD his God, as the heart of David his father had been" (1 Kings 11:4). As a result, God decrees that the kingdom will soon be divided. Israel is never again the same. It is a sad finish to a remarkable life.

Other good stories from this part of the Bible include the following:

- Ruth, Naomi, and Boaz provide a poignant love story during the time of the judges (the book of Ruth)
- Samuel receives a call from God (1 Samuel 3)
- David defeats Goliath (1 Samuel 17)
- The strong bonds of friendship between David and Saul's son Jonathan (1 Samuel 20)
- David spares Saul's life — twice! (1 Samuel 24, 26)
- Saul visits a medium at Endor (1 Samuel 28)
- The death of Absalom (2 Samuel 18)
- Solomon suggests cutting a baby in half (1 Kings 3:16–28)
- The queen of Sheba visits Solomon (1 Kings 10:1–13)

We will pick up the action of the Bible from this point in chapter 6. But first, let's look at some classic literature of the time.

FIVE

Wisdom Literature
Songs, Stories, Sayings, and Sex

We have been following the action of the Bible from Creation to the unification of the twelve tribes into a prosperous nation. Now we're going to pause to quickly examine some of the exquisite writings of the Bible.

The Book of Job
The story of Job is a distinctive book among the other sixty-five in the Bible. While the other Wisdom books are songs, sayings, and expressions of an author, the book of Job is a narrative of a man who appears to have lived during the times of the patriarchs.

Job is exemplary in his righteousness—so much so that God notes, "There is no one on earth like him." But Satan challenges God's claim, saying that since

God has blessed Job with so much, *of course* he has no trouble living a "blameless and upright" life (Job 1:8). Satan asks to take away everything Job has.

So one day a series of messengers arrives at Job's home, each with tragic news. Sabeans have carried off all his oxen and donkeys. A fire has burned up the sheep and his servants. Chaldean raiding parties have taken all his camels. And even worse, Job's ten children have all died in a sudden desert storm.

Job, of course, is devastated, yet he "did not sin by charging God with wrongdoing" (Job 1:22). When God points this out, Satan scoffs and says that if Job's health is affected, then he will crack. So Job is afflicted with painful sores over his entire body. He sits among the ashes and scrapes himself with pieces of broken pottery. His wife is no help. Her advice: "Curse God and die!" But Job has a different outlook: "Shall we accept good from God, and not trouble?" (Job 2:9–10).

All this happens in the first two chapters of the book of Job. Then, for the next thirty-five chapters, Job is visited by four friends and they discuss why he is suffering. They insist that he must have done something wrong, which he persistently denies. Yet he can't understand (much less explain) his dire circumstances.

Finally, God appears, and he and Job dialogue. (More accurately, God talks and Job listens.) Through a lengthy series of questions, God demonstrates that there is much that Job doesn't understand about life on earth. Job realizes that God is in charge, and he is content with that knowledge. And God gives Job "twice as much as he had before" and another family (Job 42:10). Job dies at age 140, "old and full of years" (Job 42:17).

The Book of Psalms

The book of Psalms is a collection of songs from a number of sources and are used for various purposes. The 150 psalms make up the longest book in the Bible. About half of them are attributed to David, two to Solomon, one to Moses, and several to various other writers. Forty-nine of them remain anonymous.

An emphasis of the Psalms is praise to God. Some are personal and confessional. Others are appropriate for public and group use, including Psalms 120–134. It is thought that these "songs of ascent" were used in temple worship and perhaps by travelers making a pilgrimage "up" to Jerusalem.

The most familiar psalm is probably Psalm 23 (see page 99). The longest one is Psalm 119, at 176 verses. The shortest is Psalm 117, at only 2 verses. Psalm 22 was quoted in part by Jesus on the cross and is one of seventeen specifically messianic psalms.

Whether expressing thanksgiving, sorrow, frustration, or joy, the Psalms are very open and honest expressions to God. Many are surprisingly bold in their frankness.

The Book of Proverbs

One of the key themes of Proverbs is wisdom, so it is no surprise that Solomon is believed to be a major contributor, yet other wise people contributed as well.

Parts of the book are essay-like writings about various topics: exhortations to embrace wisdom (Proverbs 1:8–4:27); admonitions against adultery and folly (Proverbs 5–7); qualities of "a wife of noble character" (Proverbs 31:10–31); and so on. Other portions contain long lists of not necessarily related wise sayings.

Some of our common sayings find their roots in Proverbs. For example:

- He who spares the rod hates his son, but he who loves him is careful to discipline him.
  (Proverbs 13:24)
- A gentle answer turns away wrath, but a harsh word stirs up anger. (Proverbs 15:1)
- Pride goes before destruction, a haughty spirit before a fall. (Proverbs 16:18)
- Train a child in the way he should go, and when he is old he will not turn from it. (Proverbs 22:6)

Other proverbs are more obscure, yet no less pointed:

- Like a gold ring in a pig's snout is a beautiful woman who shows no discretion. (Proverbs 11:22)
- Better to live on a corner of the roof than share a house with a quarrelsome wife. (Proverbs 21:9). (And with 700 wives, Solomon should know!)
- If a man loudly blesses his neighbor early in the morning, it will be taken as a curse. (Proverbs 27:14)

Proverbs is a good book to skim through when time permits. You're likely to be a bit wiser once you do.

The Book of Ecclesiastes

"'Meaningless! Meaningless!' says the Teacher. 'Utterly meaningless! Everything is meaningless'" (Ecclesiastes 1:1).

And with that jolly opening, the book of Ecclesiastes begins. Many believe the Teacher to be Solomon. If not, it was someone in a similar position of wealth, power, and opportunity.

The writer leads a determined search for meaning in life. He seeks meaning in pleasure: "I denied myself nothing my eyes desired" (Ecclesiastes 2:10). Yet he finds no satisfaction. He tries working hard, only to realize he will die and leave everything to someone else who hasn't worked for it (Ecclesiastes 2:21). He tries a number of pursuits, only to find them to be "meaningless, a chasing after the wind" (Ecclesiastes 2:26).

Eventually, he decides that the best anyone can do is "to eat and drink, and to find satisfaction in his toilsome labor" (Ecclesiastes 5:18). And his final conclusion? "Fear God and keep his commandments, for this is the whole duty of man" (Ecclesiastes 12:13). Acknowledgment of God's presence and involvement can add meaning to life when nothing else does.

The Song of Songs

From the frequently despondent and perplexing book of Ecclesiastes we come to the Song of Songs, which provides an altogether different experience. This writing, also attributed to Solomon, is a bold and sometimes explicit love story. It is structured as a dialogue between the Beloved (the girl)and the Lover (the guy), with occasional commentary from friends).

Among the more graphic passages is the Lover's comment: "Your stature is like that of the palm, and your breasts like clusters of fruit. I said, 'I will climb the palm tree; I will take hold of its fruit'" (Song of Songs 7:7–8). (Some Bible passages don't need much expert interpretation.)

But more true to the book as a whole is one of its closing comments:

> *Love is as strong as death,*
> > *its jealousy unyielding as the grave.*
> *It burns like blazing fire,*
> > *like a mighty flame.*
> *Many waters cannot quench love;*
> > *rivers cannot wash it away.*
> *If one were to give*
> > *all the wealth of his house for love,*
> *it would be utterly scorned.* (SONG OF SONGS 8:6–7)

Some people interpret the Song of Songs to be symbolic of the relationship between God and his people (whether Israel or the church). Perhaps it is. But it also stands alone as a lasting and classic song of love, wisdom, and romance.

A few short summaries can't do justice to the beautiful poetry and sentiment expressed in these biblical writings. But since this is a one-hour overview of the Bible, we must return to the action of the Old Testament... bleak though it is.

SIX

Divided and Conquered

The Fall of the Nation
and the Rise of the Prophets

Well, we've hit the high point of the Old Testament, and it's pretty much downhill from here. Now we begin a long, extended spiritual slide with tragic (though not unforeseen) results.

A Kingdom Divided Against Itself

(I KINGS 12–2; KINGS 25)

After Solomon sets aside all his wisdom to forsake God in favor of his many wives, it doesn't take long for the kingdom to begin to crumble. One of Solomon's officers, Jeroboam, rebels and soon becomes king of the ten-plus tribes that make up the northern kingdom (Israel). But because of David's previous faithfulness, God ensures that a portion of the nation remains in the family. Solomon's son Rehoboam becomes king of the tribe of Judah and a portion of the territory of Benjamin (known collectively as Judah). From this point on, the kingdom is divided, with each part having a succession of about twenty kings over the next 200 to 350 years.

After Saul, David, and Solomon, the kings of Israel and Judah are for the most part ineffective and inconsequential. All that is recorded for many of them is: "He did evil in the eyes of the LORD." In fact, as soon as the kingdom splits and Jeroboam sees the allure of the temple in Judah, he sets up a couple of golden calves in the northern kingdom to keep the people from feeling the need to go to Jerusalem to offer sacrifices. The God-given Mosaic Law is quickly forgotten.

And Judah does little better than Israel at maintaining a shred of spiritual integrity. Both kingdoms grow weak and vulnerable. The northern tribes are conquered and exiled to Assyria in 722 BC. The people of Judah hold out almost another century and a half before falling and being carted off to Babylon in 586 BC. But the sieges are awful, with priests slaughtered and starving mothers reduced to cannibalism of their own children (Lamentations 2:20, 4:9–10).

Ahab and Jezebel
(1 KINGS 16:29–22:40; 2 KINGS 9:30–37)

Sadly, it is the evil kings who are remembered more than the decent ones from this period of biblical history. Not too many people recall Jehoshaphat (1 Kings 22:41–50), Jotham (2 Kings 15:32–38), Hezekiah (2 Kings 18–20), or Josiah (2 Kings 22:1–23:30), who went against the tide of the time and were relatively righteous and faithful.

Instead, we hear more about Ahab and Jezebel: "There was never a man like Ahab, who sold himself to do evil in the eyes of the LORD, urged on by Jezebel his wife" (1 Kings 21:25). They worship Baal and Asherah rather than God. They make life very difficult for the prophet Elijah. And when a simple man named Naboth refuses to sell them a vineyard they want, they frame him and have him stoned to death for a false charge.

Elijah prophesied that for murdering an innocent man, both Ahab and Jezebel will be devoured by dogs, and his prophecies come to pass.

Elijah and Elisha (1 KINGS 17–2; KINGS 13:21)

When the kings of Israel and Judah stop providing spiritual leadership for the nations, God sends prophets to proclaim his truth to the people. Elijah and Elisha are bright spots in the spiritual darkness of the series of evil kings. Not only does God provide for them in unusual ways—such as being fed by ravens (1 Kings 17:1–6)—but they also receive power to perform all kinds of miracles: making lost ax heads float, calling fire from heaven, healing leprosy, and even bringing back people from the dead. At the end of his years of faithful service, Elijah is taken to heaven in a chariot of fire (2 Kings 2:1–18).

Numerous prophets are mentioned by name in the Bible, Elijah and Elisha being two of the more prominent ones. Others wrote books to record the events and messages of their ministries. The writers of the longer books are known as the Major Prophets (Isaiah, Jeremiah, Ezekiel, and Daniel). Those with shorter writings are called Minor Prophets.

Isaiah

Isaiah describes a magnificent vision he has when God first calls him to be a prophet (Isaiah 6). His outlook on the future includes both short-term events (the fall of Israel to the Assyrians and the eventual fall of Judah to the Babylonians) and long-range prophecies about the coming Messiah. Some of his more popular messianic predictions are found in Isaiah 7:14, 9:2–7, 11:1–9, and 53:1–12. His writings are frequently quoted in the New Testament.

Jeremiah

Jeremiah is sometimes called "the weeping prophet." His message of coming judgment is not a popular one. At least once his scroll of prophecies is burned (Jeremiah 36). At times people threaten his life if he doesn't quit prophesying (Jeremiah 11:18–23); another time he is tossed into a pit and left to die, but a friend helps him escape (Jeremiah 38:1–13).

And if Jeremiah's life weren't sad enough, his name comes up most often as the author of the book of Lamentations, a series of five laments detailing the fall of Jerusalem. Yet Jeremiah remains faithful and weathers the many storms of his long and dedicated life.

Ezekiel

Like Isaiah, Ezekiel has an amazing vision of God in his heaven and an unmistakable call to serve as a prophet (Ezekiel 1–2). He is among the captives carried off to Babylon, and he ministers to his people there. One of the most remarkable of Ezekiel's many visions is of a valley filled with dry bones. But when God's breath enters the bones, they are once again covered with tendons, flesh, and skin. The vision is a promise that God will restore his people and return them to Israel—no matter how hopeless their situation looks at the time (Ezekiel 37:1–14).

Daniel

Daniel is also taken into captivity. He has a God-given ability to interpret dreams, which keeps him in favor with a series of kings: Nebuchadnezzar and Belshazzar of Babylon, and Darius the Mede. Most people know about his lions' den incident (Daniel 6), which occurs late in his life. He also interprets Nebuchadnezzar's dream of an enormous statue felled by a "rock cut out of a mountain, but not by human hands" (Daniel 2:45)—a foretelling of the coming of Jesus. He later interprets mysterious writing on the wall (Daniel 5). In Daniel's book we also read the story of his friends Shadrach, Meshach, and Abednego, and their ordeal in the fiery furnace (Daniel 3). And the last half of the book (Daniel 7–12) contains prophecies that many people use to help interpret Revelation and explain the expected events of the end times.

The Minor Prophets

The Minor Prophets are Hosea, Joel, Amos, Obadiah, Jonah, Micah, Nahum, Habakkuk, Zephaniah, Haggai, Zechariah, and Malachi. Of these dozen men, the best known is Jonah because of his fascinating story of surviving three days in the belly of a great fish. Hosea's life is also interesting because he marries an adulterous woman who later leaves him and has kids with other men. Still, he takes her back to demonstrate God's persistent faithfulness to his people. Micah tells us where to look for the Messiah to be born (Micah 5:2).

And the other Minor Prophets have valuable insights into both their own times and the times to come.

The writings of the prophets are probably some of the least-read in the Bible. Yet their contribution to both their people and the totality of the Bible should never be underestimated. Though largely unknown to today's population, they all provide testimony to God's grace and mercy . . . even in the worst of times.

SEVEN

Back Home

The Return to Jerusalem

The Bible doesn't say a lot about the people who were taken to Assyria after their exile, although the spiritual reasons for their deportation are clearly listed (2 Kings 17). We read that the leader of Assyria carried them away and replaced them with people from Arab countries. But considerably more is said of the people from Judah who were taken to Babylon.

If you happen to be following along in a Bible as you read this book, you will notice that a couple of chapters back, we skipped over a few Bible books. The books of 1 and 2 Chronicles were not referenced because they contain much of the same content as the books of Samuel and Kings. But we saved the books of Ezra, Nehemiah, and Esther for this point. Chronologically, the events of those books took place during and after the people of Judah went into captivity—some of the final events of the Old Testament.

Esther

Ladies first: let's look at Esther. Her story takes place during the exile, and the other stories occur slightly later.

The Babylonians have conquered Judah, but not long afterward, the Medes and Persians then defeat the Babylonians. A ruler named Xerxes comes to power. His wife defies him one day, so he banishes her and begins a search for a new queen.

Esther has a relative named Mordecai who advises her to attempt to become queen. She does, and she is chosen above all the other hopeful contenders. But Xerxes doesn't know she is a Jew.

As it turns out, one of Xerxes' top officials, Haman, is plotting to annihilate the Jews. Esther learns of the plot and, at risk of her life, approaches the king to ask if she can schedule a dinner party for Haman. Xerxes is glad to grant her request. Later, on the very night that Haman is planning to get the king's permission to eliminate all Jews, Esther reveals her ethnicity and tells Xerxes: "I and my people have been sold for destruction and slaughter and annihilation" (Esther 7:4). Xerxes is furious, and Haman is hanged that night.

The Jewish feast of Purim commemorates this event. Although the name of God is never mentioned in the book of Esther, the many "coincidental" events and ironies of the story reflect his presence and protection.

Ezra

The prophet Jeremiah had foretold that the Israelites' captivity in Babylon would last only 70 years (Jeremiah 25:11–12, 29:10–14). After Persia defeats Babylon, the Persian king, Cyrus, is inclined to let the Jewish captives return to their homeland. In fact, Cyrus allows everyone to leave who wants to and even returns many of the furnishings that had been taken from their temple.

The problem is that the temple has been destroyed. So one of the first tasks of the returning Israelites is to rebuild it. Among the first groups to return to Israel is a man named Zerubbabel, who has been appointed governor. His group faces considerable opposition from the people who have settled in the area, yet they persevere and rebuild the temple. Ezra is a priest who comes with a subsequent group of exiles to help attend to the task. A joyful dedication and celebration follow the completion of the rebuilt temple (Ezra 6:16–22).

But it was brought to Ezra's attention that many of the men, including certain priests, have intermarried with nonbelieving women. Ezra calls for a period of confession and repentance, which is followed by the discovery that over 100 people have married foreign wives. These men agree to divorce their nonbelieving wives and send them away, along with their children.

Nehemiah

Nehemiah returns to his homeland in yet another caravan. His group sets out to rebuild the walls around Jerusalem. They, too, face a number of troublemakers who try to thwart their efforts, going so far as to make attempts on Nehemiah's life. Nehemiah is both faithful and practical, so "we prayed to our God and posted a guard day and night to meet this threat" (Nehemiah 4:9).

After the city walls are completed, Ezra assembles the people and reads from the Mosaic Law as "all the people listened attentively" (Nehemiah 8:3). The people weep as they realize how they have disregarded God's law for so long. But Ezra and Nehemiah tell them to eat and rejoice because the event is a celebration. So they feast and worship for more than a week. It is the biggest celebration they have held since the days of Joshua, "and their joy was very great" (Nehemiah 8:17–18).

Between the Testaments

As the Old Testament closes, the Hebrew people are allowed to return to their homeland, though they are still under Persian rule. About four centuries pass between the close of the Old Testament and the start of the New Testament. During that time, the Greeks defeat the Persians just as the Persians had conquered the Babylonians. However, the Greeks want to hellenize the world: unify all territories under Greek language and Greek customs.

One particularly headstrong leader named Antiochus IV Epiphanes takes a personal interest in seeing that all Jewish writings and customs are destroyed. But he pushes too hard. One Jewish family rises up in defiance, and others follow. The elder of the family is named Mattathias and has five sons. The oldest, Judas (Maccabeus), gave name to the Maccabean revolt that lasted from 166 BC to 142 BC. The Jewish people are victorious and earn their independence.

But soon the Roman Empire comes to power. After a lengthy siege, in 63 BC the Romans take over Jerusalem, slaughter priests, and defile the Most Holy Place in the temple. So, as the New Testament begins, many of the Jewish people still feel a lot of animosity toward Rome. Keep that in mind as we continue our journey through the Bible.

EIGHT

Jesus

His Humanity

Throughout the Old Testament—especially during bad times—the people were told to expect a Messiah. For centuries, God's people had been watching and waiting for a Savior. Now, with the oppression they are feeling from Rome, no doubt some of them recall the many promises that God would send someone to help.

In the flow of Bible history, everything points to the life, death, and resurrection of Jesus. Many previous events and prophecies have foreshadowed this, and everything afterward will point back to the significance of Jesus, the Messiah, the Christ ("anointed one").

Jesus' Birth (MATTHEW 1–2; LUKE 1–2)

The first we see of Jesus in the Bible, he doesn't look much like the Savior of the world. God chooses to send him to earth as a baby, to live and grow just as any other human being would.

A young girl named Mary is chosen to give birth to Jesus. The angel Gabriel appears to explain to her what is going on. She is quite confused, because she is a virgin. But Gabriel assures her that "nothing is impossible with God" (Luke 1:37). An angel also has to appear to Joseph, because when Mary turns up pregnant, he is about to "divorce" her quietly. (Although Mary and Joseph were only engaged at the time, engagements then were much more binding than are those today.) Both Mary and Joseph do as instructed and await the birth of Jesus without having any sexual contact in the meantime (Matthew 1:24–25).

The Bible does not support many of our Christmas traditions. We do know that Mary and Joseph left Nazareth to go to Bethlehem because of a Roman-ordered census. (No doubt they were glad to get out of town during the final stage of her pregnancy to avoid local gossip.) And we know that when Jesus was born, Mary and Joseph laid him in a manger. But we don't know that he was in a stable; it might have been a cave. (All we do know is that the inn was full.) We know shepherds visited him, as well as magi from the East. But when the wise men got there, Jesus was in a house, so they weren't likely kneeling around the manger with the shepherds. We aren't told how many wise men came, only that they presented the child with three gifts.

Yet it seems clear that God was alerting certain segments of the world that something earthshaking was taking place. An army of angels fills the sky to direct the shepherds to the manger. A star points the way for the magi. And when Jesus' parents present him at the temple, two people separately approach them with prophecies about what the child will do (Luke 2:25–38).

The Bible says little about Jesus' childhood, but the few clues we have indicate that he was an extraordinary person. Even at the age of 12, he was able to hold the attention of the religious leaders in the temple, causing all who hear him to be amazed (Luke 2:41–52)

Jesus' Baptism and Temptation
(MATTHEW 3:1–4:11)

The prophet Malachi had told the world to watch for the prophet Elijah to appear "before that great and dreadful day of the LORD comes" (Malachi 4:5). Isaiah had predicted a voice in the desert calling, "Prepare the way for the LORD" (Isaiah 40:3). Jesus would later identify this "Elijah" as John the Baptist (Matthew

11:11–15), who prepared the way for Jesus by preaching in the desert, calling people to repentance, and alerting them that "the kingdom of heaven is near" (Matthew 3:1–2).

We next see Jesus at age 30, coming to John to be baptized. John is reluctant at first but does as Jesus asks. As Jesus comes up out of the water, the Spirit of God descends like a dove. "And a voice from heaven said, 'This is my Son, whom I love; with him I am well pleased'" (Matthew 3:16–17).

Jesus is then led by the Spirit into the wilderness, where he fasts for 40 days and is tempted. Three times Satan tries to persuade Jesus to do something wrong or self-centered, and each time Jesus responds with an appropriate quote from the Old Testament that rebuffs Satan.

Jesus' Relationships

Jesus' nontraditional yet authoritative teaching style quickly attracts followers. He spends a night in prayer (Luke 6:12–16) and then chooses twelve of his followers to be apostles (specially commissioned disciples). Among the twelve are some who had been disciples of John the Baptist. Jesus then begins to reiterate John's message: "Repent, for the kingdom of heaven is near" (Matthew 4:17).

The twelve apostles are Simon (whom Jesus named Peter), Andrew, James, John, Philip, Bartholomew (Nathanael), Matthew (Levi), Thomas, James (the son of Alphaeus), Simon the Zealot, Thaddaeus (also identified as Judas, son of James), and Judas Iscariot.

Over his 3-year ministry, Jesus develops a bond with this circle of friends. He is especially close to Peter, James, and John, who accompany him at times when the others aren't around—such as at his Transfiguration (more on this in chapter 10) and in the Garden of Gethsemane just before his arrest.

What the Bible reveals about Jesus' relationships is frequently surprising. He is usually at odds with the religious leaders of his day (particularly the Pharisees and Sadducees). But when a Pharisee named Nicodemus comes to see him one night, he and Jesus have a fascinating conversation (John 3).

Zacchaeus, a despised tax collector, changes his cheating ways after a single dinner with Jesus (Luke 19:1–10). Jews and Gentiles alike are amazed at Jesus' willingness to help and heal them.

Jesus has great respect for women. Several follow him in his travels. Mary and Martha are close friends. The Samaritan woman at the well (John 4) is stunned that any man would even speak to her, yet her conversation with Jesus initiates a spiritual revival in her village. A woman caught in the act of adultery is brought to Jesus, primarily to force him to pass judgment on her. He refuses to condemn her, yet he cautions her to "go now and leave your life of sin" (John 8:1–11).

Even little children receive the comfort and compassion of Jesus. The disciples try to keep the kids out of the way, but Jesus scolds the adults and says, "The kingdom of heaven belongs to such as these" (Matthew 19:13–14). The self-proclaimed "experts" don't get much respect from Jesus, but those with childlike faith are always welcome.

Jesus' Emotions

The humanity of Jesus is also reflected in his wide range of emotions. He weeps at the death of his friend Lazarus (John 11:35). He gets angry and distressed when people use religious law in an attempt to trap him and disregard humanity as they do (Mark 3:1–6). His anger grows into righteous indignation on at least one occasion: he makes a whip and drives animals and money changers from the temple (John 2:12–17).

But mostly, he seems to enjoy life and appreciate people. Numerous times we read of his compassion going out to a person or group. And apparently Jesus attends so many parties with "sinners" that the religious authorities accuse him of being "a glutton and a drunkard" (Matthew 11:18–19).

According to the Bible, Jesus' humanity serves many purposes. Because he shared every human weakness and temptation that we do, he is well qualified to serve as our "high priest" and give us access to God (Hebrews 4:14–16). He understands our pain when we suffer (Philippians 3:7–10). But most of all, as we look at Jesus, we see what God is like. He is not just a list of rules and laws. He isn't a condemning and vengeful thunderbolt thrower. The love and compassion Christ shows to people reflect God's feelings for us.

Because of Jesus' humanity, "anyone who has seen me has seen the Father" (John 14:9).

NINE

Jesus

His Teachings

People have a vast number of opinions about Jesus: whether or not he was God, whether or not he actually died and came back to life, and to what degree he was superior to other prophets and religious leaders. But almost everyone agrees that he was an exceptional teacher. So let's look briefly at a number of things he taught.

The Sermon on the Mount (MATTHEW 5–7)

Jesus' Sermon on the Mount presents a phenomenally different way to approach life. Jesus affirms: "Do not think that I have come to abolish the Law or the Prophets; I have not come to abolish them but to fulfill them" (Matthew 5:17). Yet his interpretation of the Scriptures and the challenges he puts forth are different from anything people have ever heard.

He begins with the Beatitudes—statements of blessedness (see pages 99–100). He teaches that people are blessed who are poor in spirit . . . mournful . . . meek . . . merciful . . . pure in heart . . . peacemakers . . . who hunger and thirst for righteousness . . . and who are persecuted because of that righteousness (Matthew 5:3–10). Followers of God, he said, are like the salt of the earth and the light of the world, and they should be a positive influence on those around them.

Jesus teaches that murder begins with anger, and adultery with lust. And he discourages any further hatred of enemies, calling on his listeners to love their enemies instead.

It is in the Sermon on the Mount that we find the Lord's Prayer (Matthew 6:9–13) (see pages 100–101). In addition, our faith should negate much worry, and our concern should be more for storing "treasures in heaven" than for the accumulation of possessions (Matthew 6:20).

Jesus instructs us not to judge others, yet he also says to watch out for false prophets who "come to you in sheep's clothing, but inwardly they are ferocious wolves" (Matthew 7:15). And he says that those who are wise will listen to what he says and be like one who builds his house (life) on rock rather than sand.

Jesus' Parables

Although the Sermon on the Mount is clear and simple to understand (if not to apply), Jesus also uses parables in his teaching. His parables are simple stories that carry a weighty religious meaning for those with the faith to understand (Mark 4:10–12, 33–34). Those without spiritual discernment will be unable to understand to the same degree as believers.

Jesus' parables refer to things that are common in first-century Israel: seeds, fishing nets, sheep, fig trees, and such. The most popular parables seem to pertain to relationships. Two of his best-known parables are the stories of the prodigal son (Luke 15:11–32) and the Good Samaritan (Luke 10:30–37).

Even in the parable format, it's hard to miss the main points of these stories: a fresh perspective of God as a compassionate, forgiving father, and a higher standard for how we should interact with one another. These two parables emphasize what Jesus says are the greatest commandments of all: to love God wholeheartedly and to love one's neighbor as oneself (Matthew 22:34–40).

Jesus versus the Religious Authorities

Reading through the Gospels, we see that sometimes Jesus can be downright confrontational. Many of his teachings are unabashedly bold. He calls his disciples to a deeper commitment to him—above family and everything else (Luke 9:57–62). He is clear that following him will require "taking up a cross" (Matthew 10:37–39). He speaks of suffering and death as common expectations (Matthew 10:17–20, 28). And at times his frank, uncompromising teachings cause many potential followers to walk away.

But perhaps his boldest statements are reserved for the religious leaders who continually oppose him. If Jesus heals someone on the Sabbath, they overlook the fact that a suffering person is no longer in pain. Rather, they accuse Jesus of "working" on the Sabbath—an infraction of their law. Time after time they set up situations to try to trap him. But Jesus always sees through their sneakiness and puts them in their place.

It has gotten to the point where the law, as interpreted and applied by the religious leaders, seems little more than a long list of rules and regulations. The aspect of developing a relationship with God has been downplayed to the point of nonexistence. One time Jesus even berates the Pharisees with a long series of "woes," listing their offenses and calling them "blind guides," "hypocrites," "snakes," and a "brood of vipers" (Matthew 23). Whenever Jesus sees people in authority leading others to sin or twisting God's truth for their own advantage, he calls them on it. Once he has a young child come forward and says, "If anyone causes one of these little ones who believe in me to sin, it would be better for him to have a large millstone hung around his neck and to be drowned in the depths of the sea" (Matthew 18:1–6).

Some people dwell primarily on the harsh or difficult sayings of Jesus, and they reach inaccurate, perhaps even twisted, opinions about him. But taken as a whole, Jesus' teachings are a fascinating body of work, calling his listeners to a more involved life and assuring them that rewards are in store for those who devote themselves to God.

TEN

Jesus
His Divinity

I f Jesus had done little more than spend his three public years of ministry teaching and relating to people, he still would probably be one of the most talked-about figures in history. His outlook on life, his unbridled compassion for the losers of society, and his nonviolent yet direct confrontations with pompous or misguided religious authorities are enough to seal his place in the history books. But the Bible records many other things he did—things to indicate he is more than just a quirky and well-regarded human being. If Jesus' claims are true, he is indeed God.

Jesus' Miracles

The power of God is evident through Jesus' miracles. Nothing seems beyond his ability. His first miracle is changing water to wine—the best wine—at a wedding ceremony (John 2:1–11). He heals all manner of diseases: blindness, deafness, blood and other internal disorders, leprosy, withered hands, lameness, and more. He casts out demons that have powerful control over people.

He can heal with a touch. He can heal by spitting into the dirt and making a mud poultice (John 9:1–7). At times his healing doesn't require any contact at all. This is the case with the paralyzed servant of a Roman centurion. The servant is suffering terribly, and Jesus volunteers to go heal him, but the centurion asks Jesus to just "say the word, and my servant will be healed." Jesus is amazed at the man's faith and does as he has been asked. The servant is healed even though he is at a distance (Matthew 8:5–13).

Another time a woman who has been ill for 12 years approaches Jesus from behind as he walks by and touches the edge of his cloak, believing that she will be healed. She is, but Jesus realizes what has happened and stops to acknowledge her faith (Luke 8:43–48).

Jesus can instantly still a raging storm with a curt command (Mark 4:35–41). He can walk on water and even inspires one of his disciples to do so on one occasion (Matthew 14:22–33). At least twice he feeds thousands of people with an amount of food that should feed only one or two (Matthew 14:13–21, 15:29–38). Nothing seems beyond his range of power: Not disease. Not nature. Not the spiritual world. Not even death.

The Bible provides accounts of three dead people who come back to life at Jesus' command. Two are described with little commentary: the son of a widow in the town of Nain (Luke 7:11–17) and the daughter of Jairus (Luke 8:41–42, 49–56). The third resurrection is a bit more detailed. Jesus is called to attend to Lazarus, who is very ill. But rather than rush to his friend's side, he waits awhile. By the time Jesus arrives, Lazarus has been dead for 4 days. When Jesus calls for Lazarus to arise from his grave, "the dead man came out, his hands and feet wrapped with strips of linen, and a cloth around his face" (John 11:44).

Jesus' Bold Claims

Jesus' power demonstrates the power of God, and in addition he makes a number of clear statements to confirm it. Early in his ministry, Jesus frequently heals someone and then asks the person not to let anyone know (a request that the person rarely honors). But later, as he senses the time of his death approaching, he grows bolder in his statements—most often to his disciples, but occasionally to a wider group.

Among other statements, Jesus refers to himself as the "bread of life" (John 6:35), the "light of the world" (John 8:12), and the "good shepherd [who] lays down his life for the sheep" (John 10:11–12). He says, "I tell you the truth, before Abraham was born, I am!" (John 8:58). And just before his arrest and death, he tells the disciples: "I am the way and the truth and the life. No one comes to the Father except through me. If you really knew me, you would know my Father as well. From now on, you do know him and have seen him. . . . Anyone who has seen me has seen the Father" (John 14:6–7, 9).

At Jesus' trial after his arrest in Gethsemane, the high priest asks him directly: "I charge you under oath by the living God: Tell us if you are the Christ, the Son of God." Jesus replies, "Yes, it is as you say. But I say to all of you: In the future you will see the Son of Man sitting at the right hand of the Mighty One and coming on the clouds of heaven" (Matthew 26:63–64).

Jesus' Transfiguration (LUKE 9:28–36)

In addition to Jesus' miracles and his outright claims to be God, three of his disciples are witness to another amazing event. Peter, James, and John are with Jesus when he is "transfigured before them" (Matthew 17:2). The biblical description is succinct but startling: "As he was praying, the appearance of his face changed, and his clothes became as bright as a flash of lightning. Two men, Moses and Elijah, appeared in glorious splendor, talking with Jesus. They spoke about his departure, which he was about to bring to fulfillment at Jerusalem" (Luke 9:29–31). A voice from heaven is also heard: "This is my Son, whom I have chosen; listen to him" (Luke 9:35).

Jesus' Death and Resurrection

But the most convincing proof of Jesus' claims to be God, in addition to the miracles he performs, and in addition to the astounding events witnessed by those closest to him, is his own resurrection. After being sold out to the authorities by Judas Iscariot for thirty pieces of silver and betrayed by a kiss, Jesus is arrested. He undergoes a quick series of trials and is convicted of blasphemy: claiming to be God (Matthew 26:57–66). He is beaten, slapped, and spat on. A crown of thorns is shoved onto his head. The Roman governor, Pontius Pilate, is reluctant to convict him but finally gives in to the pressure of the crowds.

Jesus is made to carry his own cross to Golgotha (Calvary), "the Place of the Skull." He is then nailed to that cross and hangs, naked, while soldiers gamble for his clothing—all that he owns. From the cross Jesus forgives his tormentors, promises a fellow crucifixion victim a home in paradise, and cries out to God.

Crucifixion was a horrendous way to die. It was intended to be a slow and torturous death, sometimes taking days. But within a few hours of being nailed to the cross, Jesus dies. A spear is thrust into his side to ensure that he is dead.

The Romans and the Jewish religious authorities hope that will be the end of things. But they know Jesus had said he would rise on the third day after his death, so they roll a large stone over his grave, seal it, and post a guard.

Yet 3 days later, when a group of women arrive to anoint Jesus' body, they find the stone moved and the grave empty. A radiant angel had appeared during the night, rolled back the stone, and sat on it. The courageous soldiers of the Roman Empire are "so afraid of him that they shook and became like dead men" (Matthew 28:4). The guards apparently fled, but the Jewish religious authorities later bribed them to say that they had dozed off and the disciples had stolen the body (Matthew 28:-15). They also promised to keep the soldiers out of trouble with their superiors, as Rome wouldn't tolerate soldiers sleeping on their posts.

The angel is still present when the women come early in the morning. He tells them, "[Jesus] is not here; he has risen, just as he said" (Matthew 28:6). Shortly afterward, Mary Magdalene has an encounter with Jesus himself, the first of about a dozen of his postresurrection appearances (John 20:10–18). And one of those appearances is to a group of about 500 people (1 Corinthians 15:3-8).

The Bible provides convincing evidence of the reality of Jesus' resurrection. The absence of his body from the tomb is key. When word spread that he was alive again, all the authorities would have had to do to quash the rumors was produce the body. And it is unthinkable that the cowardly disciples could have stolen a body that was in a sealed tomb under Roman guard. Even if they could have, Scripture and history tell us that ten of the remaining eleven disciples (after Judas hanged himself) died martyrs' deaths. If they had stolen the body and contrived a resurrection hoax, it certainly wouldn't have been worth dying for.

Jesus' Ascension (ACTS 1:1–11)

One final biblical event in the life of Jesus verifies his claims to divinity. The occasional appearances of Jesus take place over a period of 40 days, but on the fortieth day, he gives his disciples final instructions and then "he was taken up before their very eyes, and a cloud hid him from their sight" (Acts 1:9). The disciples continue to stare into the sky until a pair of angels appears and tells them, "This same Jesus, who has been taken from you into heaven, will come back in the same way you have seen him go into heaven" (Acts 1:11).

Many people, of course, dispute any suggestion that Jesus was more than a skilled teacher. But the Bible allows no alternative other than that he was Emmanuel ("God with us"), the promised Messiah and Savior of the world. Most of the rest of the Bible will attempt to explain and make sense of this concept.

ELEVEN

The Early Church

Among Jesus' final words to his disciples was a promise: "Do not leave Jerusalem, but wait for the gift my father promised. . . . But you will receive power when the Holy Spirit comes on you; and you will be my witnesses in Jerusalem, and in all Judea and Samaria, and to the ends of the earth" (Acts 1:4, 8). The work of the Holy Spirit and the witness of Jesus' followers is what fills the rest of the Bible, from Acts to Revelation.

Tongues of Fire (ACTS 2)

Many political and religious movements throughout history have crumbled when the leader quit, died, or otherwise stopped providing motivation and leadership. At this time the believers in Jesus number only 120 (Acts 1:15), and with their leader gone, it might be anticipated that Christianity will never come to fruition.

Yet Jesus is replaced with another God-sent leader: the Holy Spirit. One day when the believers are together, the sound of a violent wind fills the room and what looks like tongues of fire rest on each person. At that point, "all of them were filled with the Holy Spirit and began to speak in other tongues as the Spirit enabled them" (Acts 2:4).

Visiting Jerusalem at the time are "God-fearing Jews from every nation under heaven" (Acts 2:5). As it turns out, the followers of Jesus are "declaring the wonders of God" in the languages of all those people (Acts 2:11). Everyone hears about Jesus in his or her own language. Naturally, some people chalk up this unconventional event to the disciples' having too much wine. But Peter assures the crowds that is not the case. After his short sermon, "about three thousand were added to their number that day" (Acts 2:41). The believers begin a communal lifestyle, eating and worshiping together and sharing their possessions with those who are in need. And their numbers continue to grow.

Spirit-Powered People

The Holy Spirit continues to make his presence known. Empowered by the Spirit, the once-timid and unsure disciples begin to stand strong and defend their beliefs when opposed. In addition, they are given great power for healing. Jesus had once told them, "Anyone who has faith in me will do what I have been doing. He will do even greater things than these, because I am going to the Father" (John 14:12).

Peter, for example, heals a crippled beggar (Acts 3:1–10), stands up to the Sanhedrin (a sort of religious Supreme Court), has a vision that convinces him to include Gentiles as believers (Acts 10), and experiences a miraculous release from prison (Acts 12:1–19). It gets to the point where people bring sick friends and relatives into the street on mats, hoping that Peter's shadow will fall on them (Acts 5:15–16).

As the number of believers grows, the original apostles keep teaching and preaching as they bring on new leaders (deacons) to attend to the needs of the people. And even those deacons are empowered by the Holy Spirit to do great things. One of them, Philip, follows the prompting of the Spirit into the desert, where he finds an Ethiopian struggling to understand a passage in Isaiah. Philip helps the man understand and believe what he was reading and perhaps introduces the gospel to Africa by doing so.

Another deacon is Stephen, "a man full of God's grace and power" who does "great wonders and miraculous signs among the people" (Acts 6:8). He is so influential that those who oppose him provide false witnesses, arrest him, and have him stoned to death. Even then, Stephen delivers a powerful final statement about Jesus, telling the hostile crowd, "I see heaven open and the Son of Man standing at the right hand of God" (Acts 7:56). As the stones strike him, Stephen prays for forgiveness for his attackers.

Persecution from Without

Attending the stoning of Stephen (and giving his approval) is a young man named Saul, who will become the apostle Paul. But first he will become an active opponent of the spread of the new Jesus-based religion. Eventually Jesus' followers are called Christians, although this may have started out as a derogatory term (Acts 11:26).

Saul isn't the only persecutor of the believers. They are beset by opposition from numerous sources. Many experience beatings and imprisonment. James, one of Jesus' inner circle of disciples, is beheaded by Herod, who sees that "this pleased the Jews" (Acts 12:3). But Herod soon learns that he isn't in total control, as he had thought. When a group of people praise him as a god and he doesn't correct them, immediately "an angel of the Lord struck him down, and he was eaten by worms and died" (Acts 12:21–23). But his death does nothing to reduce the persecution felt by the Christians.

Problems from Within

As might be expected with any rapidly growing movement, there is no guarantee that all members of the early church are as committed as they should be. For example, one couple sell some property and say they have donated the entire proceeds to the church, when in fact they keep some of the money for themselves. It is certainly their prerogative to donate only a portion, but their intentional and surreptitious cover-up is exposed as lying to God (Acts 5:4).

Confronted by Peter, the husband drops dead where he stands. Three hours later, unaware of what has happened to her husband, the wife also insists that they have given the church everything they received from the sale of their property. She, too, dies immediately. This was a clear example that "nothing in all creation is hidden from God's sight. Everything is uncovered and laid bare before the eyes of him to whom we must give account" (Hebrews 4:13). And as a result, "great fear seized the whole church and all who heard about these events" (Acts 5:1–10).

Another man, a sorcerer, sees the power of the Holy Spirit at work and offers the disciples money to receive it. He is severely rebuked (Acts 8:9–25). Yet another sorcerer tries to oppose Paul (after his remarkable conversion) and is blinded for a length of time (Acts 13:4–12).

As time passes, various doctrines and teachings begin to drift into the church that aren't completely grounded in truth. Some of those problems will become more damaging to the church than the external persecution. Yet the Holy Spirit working through Jesus' committed followers provides power and wisdom for the early church to continue to persevere and grow.

TWELVE

Paul

His Life and Ministry

Other than Jesus, Paul is perhaps the most significant figure in the New Testament. Although Peter, John, and other of Jesus' disciples went on to have influential and lasting ministries, Paul took the gospel of Jesus to a whole new realm: the Gentile nations.

Paul's Background

In Paul's first appearance in the Bible, he isn't seen as a good guy. While Stephen is being stoned to death, Paul is watching the coats of the stone throwers and giving assent to their actions (Acts 7:57–58, 8:1). At some point his name changes from Saul to Paul, but the change isn't explained. Perhaps he took a more Gentile-sounding name when he began a ministry to those outside the Jewish faith.

But Paul is certainly a good Jewish man. He was born in Tarsus, a city rich with Greek and Roman influences. Not only was his father a Pharisee, but Paul also had the honor of being born a Roman citizen, which gave him certain privileges. And he studied under a respected rabbi named Gamaliel (Acts 22:3, 26:4–5). So when the followers of Jesus attempt to introduce new teachings to the Jews that conflict with his beliefs, Paul does all he can to arrest, imprison, and put them to death (Acts 26:9–11).

Paul's Conversion (ACTS 9:1–19, 22:1–21, 26:9–18)
One day Paul has gotten permission to go to Damascus (about 150 miles away) to seek out any believers in Jesus, planning to bring them back to Jerusalem as prisoners. But along the way, he is stopped in his tracks by a brilliant light from heaven. He falls to the ground and hears a voice ask, "Saul, Saul, why do you persecute me?" Unable to see, Paul asks, "Who are you, Lord?" The voice replies: "I am Jesus, whom you are persecuting. Now get up and go into the city, and you will be told what you must do" (Acts 9:4–6).

The men with Paul hear something but don't know what is going on. Clearly something has happened to Paul because he remains blind for 3 days. A brave and faithful disciple in Damascus named Ananias is instructed by God to restore Paul's sight and introduce him to the believers there. Ananias does as he is told, and Paul believes and is baptized. When the Jewish leaders discover that Paul has converted, they plot to kill him. Paul faces much persecution for the rest of his life.

Paul's Mission

After his conversion, Paul quickly becomes just as passionate to spread the word about Jesus as he had previously been to persecute believers. He realizes God has been preparing him for this transformation (Galatians 1:13–17). And indeed, the work of Paul is responsible for much of the New Testament. The book of Acts (written by Luke) records much about Paul's life and is followed by thirteen epistles (letters) written by Paul to various people and churches.

Soon he is called to travel with another disciple, Barnabas, and take the good news about Jesus to other places. This would be the first of three missionary journeys. Paul helps start churches, later revisiting or writing to many of them in order to keep in touch. His teaching and instructions to the churches lay the groundwork for much of the doctrinal basis for Christianity.

Paul's Suffering

Paul considers suffering for his beliefs to be not only a reasonable expectation for a Christian but also a privilege because it connects him with the suffering of Jesus. When a group of pseudoapostles attempts to usurp his authority, he gives a succinct description of some of the things he had been through:

> I have worked much harder, been in prison more frequently, been flogged more severely, and been exposed to death again and again. Five times I received from the Jews the forty lashes minus one. Three times I was beaten with rods, once I was stoned, three times I was shipwrecked, I spent a night and a day in the open sea, I have been constantly on the move. I have been in danger from rivers, in danger from bandits, in danger from my own countrymen, in danger from Gentiles; in danger in the city, in danger in the country, in danger at sea; and in danger from false brothers. I have labored and toiled and have often gone without sleep; I have known hunger and thirst and have often gone without food; I have been cold and naked. Besides everything else, I face daily the pressure of my concern for all the churches. (2 Corinthians 11:23–28)

Paul: His Later Years

Paul didn't mind arrest and imprisonment because it enabled him to share his beliefs with influential people. Late in his life he was arrested and taken to Rome for trial, after which he was released. But apparently he was arrested again, and tradition says he was beheaded. Yet he lived his life in a state of contentment (Philippians 4:12–13) and was ready to die whenever the time came. Since he was living for his Lord, he could say with confidence, "For to me, to live is Christ and to die is gain" (Philippians 1:21).

THIRTEEN

Paul

His Letters

The first five books of the New Testament have four authors. The Gospels of Matthew and John were written by two of Jesus' original twelve apostles. Mark was authored by John Mark, a young follower of Jesus. The Gospel of Luke and book of Acts were most likely written by Luke, an educated Gentile convert and occasional traveling companion of Paul. But Paul is credited with the next thirteen books—letters to churches and friends.

The order of Paul's epistles in the Bible isn't necessarily chronological. We won't worry much about the dates here since many of them are debated among Bible scholars. We'll simply follow their order in the Bible because *what* Paul wrote is worthwhile regardless of when he wrote it.

Romans

Paul's letter to the church in Rome covers so many key doctrines that it's sometimes called the Constitution of the New Testament. Paul is frank about the widespread influence of sin—"All have sinned and fall short of the glory of God" (Romans 3:23)—as well as its consequences: "The wages of sin is death" (Romans 6:23). But he is just as clear that Jesus' atoning death makes it possible for us to experience God's forgiveness, love, and mercy. He affirms: "There is now no condemnation for those who are in Christ Jesus" (Romans 8:1). Such people are "God's children" and "heirs of God and co-heirs with Christ" (Romans 8:16–17).

1 and 2 Corinthians

The letters Paul writes to the church in Corinth are considerably more personal and intimate than his epistle to the Romans. Still, they deal with numerous practical aspects of church life: church members who flaunt blatant sin, lawsuits, marriage, spiritual gifts, propriety during the Lord's Supper, speaking in tongues, resurrection of the dead, suffering, and much more. And 1 Corinthians 13 is the "love chapter" of the Bible. All or portions of it are read at many weddings (see pages 101–102).

Galatians

The Epistle to the Galatian churches is a manifesto of freedom. Legalism is already a problem in the church, and Paul makes it abundantly clear that faith in Jesus should result in freedom, spiritual liberty, and relief from the burden of keeping a long list of legal do's and don'ts. The "fruit of the Spirit" in believers' lives is "love, joy, peace, patience, kindness, goodness, faithfulness, gentleness and self-control. Against such things there is no law" (Galatians 5:22–23).

Ephesians

During his travels, Paul spent about 3 years in Ephesus (Acts 20:31). Yet rather than addressing specific problems there, Paul's letter challenges his readers to remain focused on Christ and what his sacrificial death accomplished. Paul reminds them: "For it is by grace you have been saved, through faith—and this not from yourselves, it is the gift of God—not by works, so that no one can boast. For we are God's workmanship, created in Christ Jesus to do good works, which God prepared in advance for us to do" (Ephesians 2:8–10). Believers have been chosen and sealed, and in response they should live in the light of the truth and in unity with one another. They have been given "the armor of God" to equip them to do so (Ephesians 6:10–18).

Philippians

From the confinement of prison, Paul writes the church at Philippi and challenges them to "rejoice in the Lord always. I will say it again: Rejoice!" (Philippians 4:4). The letter to the Philippians is one of the most heartening passages in the Bible. Paul encourages his readers to strive for joy, humility, thanksgiving, and unity. Paul's goal is clear: "Forgetting what is behind and straining toward what is ahead, I press on toward the goal to win the prize for which God has called me heavenward in Christ Jesus" (Philippians 3:13–14).

In addition, "Whatever is true, whatever is noble, whatever is right, whatever is pure, whatever is lovely, whatever is admirable—if anything is excellent or praiseworthy–think about such things...And the God of peace will be with you" (Philippians 4:8–9).

Colossians

Paul's letter to the Colossians is another one written while he is under arrest, but with a more serious tone than the one written to the Philippians. Heresy is spreading through the church, and Paul is trying to firmly but lovingly steer the Colossians back to the truth. In doing so, he repeatedly points to the supremacy of Christ in all things.

1 and 2 Thessalonians

As believers in Thessalonica have begun to die without seeing the promised return of Jesus, those remaining naturally have questions about the afterlife. Paul assures them that "we who are still alive, who are left till the coming of the Lord, will certainly not precede those who have fallen asleep. For the Lord himself will come down from heaven, with a loud command, with the voice of the archangel and with the trumpet call of God, and the dead in Christ will rise first. After that, we who are still alive and are left will be caught up together with them in the clouds to meet the Lord in the air" (1 Thessalonians 4:15–17). Rather than being a source of confusion and consternation for believers, the matter of death and resurrection should be cause for encouragement (1 Thessalonians 4:18).

1 and 2 Timothy

Paul's final four letters are more personal. Two are sent to Timothy, a young pastor and Paul's fellow traveler on occasion. Paul challenges Timothy to remain strong and provides some ground rules for church officers. He also encourages his young protégé, telling him, "Don't let anyone look down on you because you are young, but set an example for the believers in speech, in life, in love, in faith and in purity" (1 Timothy 4:12). In addition, Paul says, "God did not give us a spirit of timidity, but a spirit of power, of love and of self-discipline" (2 Timothy 1:7).

Titus

Like Timothy, Titus is a younger associate of Paul's. And naturally, Paul covers many of the same topics with Titus that he did with Timothy.

Philemon

This is perhaps the most unusual (and shortest) of Paul's letters. Philemon is a Christian man whose slave, Onesimus, has apparently stolen something and then run away. While a fugitive, Onesimus runs into Paul, and Paul sends the runaway back with a personal appeal to Philemon: "Perhaps the reason he was separated from you for a little while was that you might have him back for good—no longer as a slave, but better than a slave, as a dear brother" (Philemon 1:15–16).

Any of Paul's letters can be a good source for Bible study–close examination and personal application. We certainly haven't done them justice in this short chapter, but be assured that Paul's first-century writings continue to inspire and influence thousands of people today.

FOURTEEN

Other New Testament Letters

As we saw in the last two chapters, the apostle Paul was a busy guy with all his missionary traveling and letter writing. But during the rapid growth of the early church, all of the church leaders stayed pretty busy. In this chapter we'll look at the writings of some of the other key figures.

Hebrews

Although much speculation has been made, no one knows for sure who wrote the letter to the Hebrews. It is a distinctive work by someone well versed in both Old Testament law and the life, death, and resurrection of Jesus. Indeed, the letter is written to those familiar with Judaism, to show how the law pointed to Jesus and how Jesus fulfilled everything that was left incomplete in the law. For example, Jesus' sacrificial death was a "once for all" event to replace the annual sacrifices of bulls and goats (Hebrews 10:2, 10).

The writer contrasts Jesus with many of the people and things revered by his or her readers, including angels, prophets, Moses, and Aaron (the first high priest). In each case it is shown that Christ is superior. His role and significance in history are unique and inimitable. The author also provides a sort of Hall of Fame of heroes of faith (Hebrews 11), followed by a reminder that those people were faithful without ever seeing the promised result of their faith. Believers in Jesus, on the other hand, *have* seen (or read about) the Messiah that God had promised for centuries, and consequently, they should live their lives accordingly.

James

The most likely author for the book of James is one of Jesus' brothers. After Mary gave birth to Jesus while a virgin, she raised other sons and daughters, one of whom was James (Mark 6:2–3). And we know Jesus' brothers didn't believe in him at first (John 7:5).

But apparently James came around. He became a leader of the early church (Acts 15:12–21), and his book of the Bible is one of the most direct and practical—easy to read if not to put into practice. He calls for believers to endure suffering with joy by calling upon the wisdom of God. He emphasizes the importance of works (being doers of God's Word, and not just hearers) as a verification of one's faith—so much so that his writing was almost left out of the biblical canon.

James strongly identifies the tongue as a problem that can't be tamed, "a restless evil, full of deadly poison" (James 3:7–8). He also rebukes those who show preferential treatment to rich people over poor, especially in a church setting.

Finally, James reminds his readers of the brevity of life and the power of faith and prayer. Rather than boasting, we should make plans on the condition: "If it is the Lord's will" (James 4:13–17).

1 and 2 Peter

Peter, Jesus' close friend and disciple, wrote two short letters. He reflected several of the same themes already promoted by Paul, James, and other writers. He calls his readers to separate themselves spiritually from the secular world and devote themselves to holiness. Although believers live in this world, they should do so as "strangers" (1 Peter 1:17) and "chosen people, a royal priesthood, a holy nation, a people belonging to God" (1 Peter 2:9).

Suffering is a part of everyone's life, says Peter, so we shouldn't be surprised when it happens. Besides, those who "participate in the sufferings of Christ" should endure their troubles with joy and perseverance (1 Peter 4:12–19).

Since believers are surrounded by spiritual danger (1 Peter 5:8–9), they should keep things in perspective by remembering that Jesus has promised to return. What may seem like a long time to us, Peter says, is nothing in the scope of eternity. "With the Lord a day is like a thousand years, and a thousand years are like a day" (2 Peter 3:8). When it finally gets here, "the day of the Lord will come like a thief" (2 Peter 3:10). And we are to keep in mind the reason for the perceived delay: "The Lord is not slow in keeping his promise, as some understand slowness. He is patient with you, not wanting anyone to perish, but everyone to come to repentance" (2 Peter 3:9).

1 John, 2 John, and 3 John

In addition to the fourth Gospel, Jesus' disciple John is credited with writing three letters and the book of Revelation. John was never one to call himself by name. In his Gospel he refers to himself as "the apostle whom Jesus loved." And he doesn't identify himself in his letters, either, though there is a strong consensus that John was the author.

He addresses his readers as "my dear children," which not only has a spiritual significance but also reflects the fact that John was advanced in age when he wrote. According to church tradition, he was the only one of Jesus' eleven disciples (after Judas killed himself) to be spared a martyr's death.

John calls his readers to make good choices: Choose light over darkness (1 John 1:5–7). Love God rather than "the world or anything in the world" (1 John 2:15–17). Don't be self-centered and petty like Cain, but be loving and generous like Jesus (1 John 3:11–24).

John focuses on the importance of loving one another, and he isn't talking about a hearts-and-flowers kind of love. Indeed, love is the verification of one's relationship with Jesus: "We love because he first loved us. If anyone says, 'I love God,' yet hates his brother, he is a liar. For anyone who does not love his brother, whom he has seen, cannot love God, whom he has not seen. And he has given us this command: Whoever loves God must also love his brother" (1 John 4:19–21).

John's second and third letters are both very brief yet offer encouragement to believers and warnings about would-be deceivers (antichrists) at work among them.

Jude

The author of the book of Jude was likely another brother of Jesus named Judas (Matthew 13:55)—not

Judas Iscariot or the other disciple named Judas. His concern is that a heresy is beginning to spread within the church. He writes to remind his readers of the meaning of their salvation and to challenge them to remember the truth they have been taught.

So at this point in the Bible we are sixty-five books down and one to go. But the one that's left … it's a doozy.

FIFTEEN

Revelation
The Big Finish

Many times when someone expresses a wish to know more about the Bible, the real desire is to better comprehend the enigmatic and apocalyptic book of Revelation. This brief chapter attempts to summarize some of the symbols and content of the book, but interpreting those symbols is another matter. In fact, Bible scholars don't even agree if the things in Revelation are yet to come or have already happened (for the most part). Those who read the book as literally as possible tend to see the events as future. Those who take a more symbolic interpretation can link many of the phenomenal events described to the Roman destruction of the Jewish temple in AD 70. Whatever your opinion, Revelation is a fascinating book to read and contemplate.

Seven Letters from John's Island Exile
(REVELATION 1–3)

While Jesus' apostle John was spared a martyr's death, he was exiled for a time on the island of Patmos. While there, he had a vision of Jesus in a magnificent, glorious state (Revelation 1:12–18).

Jesus instructs John to write letters to seven churches in Asia (Revelation 2:1–3:22), each of which includes a specific reference to Jesus, an acknowledgment of what the church is doing well, problems within the church, and a promise of what will happen if the church overcomes and perseveres.

From Earth to Heaven (REVELATION 4–20)

After John records the messages to the churches, he sees a door open in heaven and hears a voice inviting him to enter. Immediately he is "in the Spirit" and has a vision of "what must take place after this" (Revelation 4:1–2). He first sees the throne of God surrounded by human elders and angelic creatures. The figure on the throne has an important scroll, but no one is worthy to open it, which causes John to weep. But then he sees "a Lamb, looking as if it had been slain," who was worthy to open the scroll (Revelation 5:6–8).

The scroll has seven seals, and as each seal is opened, John witnesses something horrific taking place on earth. At the opening of each of the first four seals, John sees a horse—each time a different color—with rider. Together these have come to be known as the four horsemen of the apocalypse, representing war, famine, conquest, and death (Revelation 6:1–8).

The seventh seal initiates a series of seven angels with trumpets, each signaling another catastrophic judgment. A "loud voice" initiates a series of "seven bowls of God's wrath" (Revelation 16:1). Among all the seals, trumpets, and bowls of wrath, John witnesses both heavenly and earthly events. He sees a great red dragon (Satan) supported by two other "beasts" (commonly referred to as the Antichrist and false prophet). The number of the beast is 666, and no one can buy or sell without the mark of the beast on his or her right hand or forehead (Revelation 13:16–18).

John also sees a great crowd of people who have been martyred, who are crying out to God for justice (Revelation 6:9–11, 7:13–17). Two witnesses with great power defy the beast and prophesy for three and a half years, after which the beast attacks and kills them. But after their bodies lie in the street for three and a half days, they come back to life, stand up, and go "up to heaven in a cloud" in full view of everyone (Revelation 11:1–12).

An enormous war breaks out at a place called Armageddon (Revelation 16:16). But while the human war is terrible in its own right, even more severe is God's judgment of people who refuse to repent. After a long series of natural disasters (undrinkable water, scorched earth, darkness, 100-pound hailstones, and such), Jesus returns with a heavenly army and puts an end to the struggles (Revelation 19:11-21).

In the end, the beast, false prophet, and Satan are thrown into "the lake of burning sulfur" where "they will be tormented day and night for ever and ever." The defiant humans are also judged and thrown into the lake of fire (Revelation 20:10–15).

A Happy (and Eternal) Ending

(REVELATION 21–22)

In welcome contrast is the conclusion of the book of Revelation. John witnesses a new heaven, a new earth, and a heavenly city where God dwells and the river of life flows. And "he who overcomes will inherit all this" (Revelation 21:7). The city has streets of gold and gates made of pearl, along with numerous other precious stones. There is no need of light or a temple because God's presence serves both purposes. In this eternal city, God "will wipe every tear from their eyes. There will be no more death or mourning or crying or pain" (Revelation 21:4).

And in the final chapter of Revelation, Jesus says no less than three times, "I am coming soon." While some may see Revelation as a threatening and worrisome work, its intent was to inspire the churches and encourage believers to remain faithful no matter what.

One thing that comes through clearly in the book of Revelation is that God is in control of earthly matters and can step in to judge and set things right at any time. Those who put their faith in him and live accordingly can anticipate a worry-free eternity with him. It's a happy ending to life...and to this one-hour whirlwind overview of the Bible.

Appendix

The Days of Creation (GENESIS 1:1–2:3)

Day 1   God creates light and separates light from darkness, establishing day and night.

Day 2   God parts the existing waters, creating an expanse between them—the sky.

Day 3   God separates the waters from the dry ground on earth, forming land and seas. The land then begins to produce vegetation: seed-bearing plants and trees.

Day 4   God places lights in the expanse of the sky: the sun, moon, and stars. The sun and moon provide light for the earth, and altogether they serve to mark days, years, and seasons.

Day 5   God creates fish to fill the seas and birds to fill the skies. Various species are created "according to their kinds" (Genesis 1:21).

Day 6   God creates land creatures and then humans to rule over (and name) the other animals.

Day 7   God rests. He blesses the seventh day (Sabbath) and declares it holy.

The Ten Commandments (EXODUS 20:1–13)

1. You shall have no other gods before me.
2. You shall not make for yourself an idol in the form of anything in heaven above or on the earth beneath or in the waters below.
3. You shall not misuse the name of the LORD your God.
4. Remember the Sabbath day by keeping it holy.
5. Honor your father and your mother, so that you may live long in the land the LORD your God is giving you.
6. You shall not murder.
7. You shall not commit adultery.
8. You shall not steal.
9. You shall not give false testimony against your neighbor.
10. You shall not covet . . . anything that belongs to your neighbor.

Notice that the first four commandments refer to a person's relationship with God. The remaining six deal with people's relationships with one another.

Psalm 23

The LORD is my shepherd, I shall not be in want.
He makes me lie down in green pastures,
*   he leads me beside quiet waters,*
*   he restores my soul.*
He guides me in paths of righteousness
*   for his name's sake.*
Even though I walk
*   through the valley of the shadow of death,*
I will fear no evil,
*   for you are with me;*
your rod and your staff,
*   they comfort me.*
You prepare a table before me
*   in the presence of my enemies.*
You anoint my head with oil;
*   my cup overflows.*
Surely goodness and love will follow me
*   all the days of my life,*
and I will dwell in the house of the LORD forever.

The Beatitudes (MATTHEW 5:3–12)

Blessed are the poor in spirit,
*   for theirs is the kingdom of heaven.*
Blessed are those who mourn,
*   for they will be comforted.*

Blessed are the meek,
     for they will inherit the earth.
Blessed are those who hunger and thirst for righteousness,
     for they will be filled.
Blessed are the merciful,
     for they will be shown mercy.
Blessed are the pure in heart,
     for they will see God.
Blessed are the peacemakers,
     for they will be called sons of God.
Blessed are those who are persecuted because of righteousness,
     for theirs is the kingdom of heaven.
Blessed are you when people insult you, persecute you
and falsely say all kinds of evil against you because of
me. Rejoice and be glad, because great is your reward
in heaven, for in the same way they persecuted the
prophets who were before you.

The Lord's Prayer (MATTHEW 6:9–13 KJV)
Our Father which art in heaven, Hallowed be thy name.
Thy kingdom come. Thy will be done in earth, as it is in
     heaven.
Give us this day our daily bread.
And forgive us our debts, as we forgive our debtors.

And lead us not into temptation, but deliver us from evil:
For thine is the kingdom, and the power, and the glory,
*   for ever.*
Amen.

The Love Chapter (1 CORINTHIANS 13)

If I speak in the tongues of men and of angels, but have not love, I am only a resounding gong or a clanging cymbal.

If I have the gift of prophecy and can fathom all mysteries and all knowledge, and if I have a faith that can move mountains, but have not love, I am nothing. If I give all I possess to the poor and surrender my body to the flames, but have not love, I gain nothing.

Love is patient, love is kind. It does not envy, it does not boast, it is not proud. It is not rude, it is not self-seeking, it is not easily angered, it keeps no record of wrongs. Love does not delight in evil but rejoices with the truth. It always protects, always trusts, always hopes, always perseveres.

Love never fails. But where there are prophecies, they will cease; where there are tongues, they will be stilled; where there is knowledge, it will pass away. For we know in part and we prophesy in part, but when perfection comes, the imperfect disappears. When I was a child, I talked like a child, I thought like a child,

I reasoned like a child. When I became a man, I put childish ways behind me. Now we see but a poor reflection as in a mirror; then we shall see face to face. Now I know in part; then I shall know fully, even as I am fully known.

And now these three remain: faith, hope and love. But the greatest of these is love.

The Books of the Bible

THE OLD TESTAMENT
Genesis
Exodus
Leviticus
Numbers
Deuteronomy
Joshua
Judges
Ruth
1 Samuel
2 Samuel
1 Kings
2 Kings
1 Chronicles
2 Chronicles
Ezra
Nehemiah
Esther
Job
Psalms
Proverbs
Ecclesiastes
Song of Songs

Isaiah
Jeremiah
Lamentations
Ezekiel
Daniel
Hosea
Joel
Amos
Obadiah
Jonah
Micah
Nahum
Habakkuk
Zephaniah
Haggai
Zechariah
Malachi

THE NEW TESTAMENT
Matthew
Mark
Luke
John

Acts
Romans
1 Corinthians
2 Corinthians
Galatians
Ephesians
Philippians
Colossians
1 Thessalonians
2 Thessalonians
1 Timothy
2 Timothy
Titus
Philemon
Hebrews
James
1 Peter
2 Peter
1 John
2 John
3 John
Jude
Revelation

ABOUT THE AUTHOR

Stan Campbell is a writer with more than twenty years of experience in youth ministry and fifteen years in Christian publishing. He is the author of numerous books and curriculum products for both youth and adults. He and his wife, Kathy, live in the Nashville area.

POCKET
BIBLE
TRIVIA

POCKET BIBLE TRIVIA

Stan Campbell

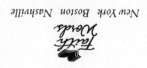
FaithWords

New York Boston Nashville

Contents

Introduction vii

1. *Identify the Quote* 1

2. *It's a Miracle!* 3

3. *Who Knows His Moses?* 6

4. *Not a Handsome Fellow* 12

5. *We Three Kings* 15

6. *Complete the Psalm* 18

7. *May I Have Your Attention, Please?* 25

8. *Complete the Proverb* 28

9. *Dreams and Visions* 33

10. *The Writing Prophets* 37

11. *Sixteen Horrible Deaths* 41

12. *The Original Christmas Story* 44

13. *The Life of Jesus* 50

14. *The Teachings of Jesus* 55

15. *Jesus' Death and Resurrection* 59

Contents

16. *A Baker's Dozen of Disciples 66*

17. *Sound Bytes 69*

18. *The Life of Paul 73*

19. *The Writings of Paul 78*

20. *Where Do Babies Come From? 83*

21. *The Bible or the Bard? 87*

Answer Key 90

Introduction

This is not a book for Bible scholars. If you have a wall covered with theology/divinity degrees or have devoted a long lifetime to the examination of every detail tucked among the thousands of lines of Scripture, thanks for your interest, but you can put this book back on the shelf.

Rather, this book is for people who may actually know very little about the contents of the Bible. Those who will get the most out of it are people who want to learn more—who are willing to ponder what they already know and look up new bits of information they discover.

This book was written with the hope that the user will have a pleasant experience reviewing his or her knowledge of Bible "trivia" (an unfortunate word, because I would not suggest that any portion of the Bible is by any means trivial). In fact, I haven't done my job if you don't stop periodically and think, *I didn't know that was in the Bible!*

So don't approach this book of Bible "trivia" with the expectation of regurgitating facts you already know. Instead, may you enjoy a voyage of discovery to see what *else* is in

the Bible to add to your existing knowledge. You are likely to find that many "trivial" portions of the Bible still contain significant life lessons for those of us trying to navigate our lives in the twenty-first century.

A short book like this can't cover everything in Scripture, but great effort has been made to include many of the usually overlooked portions in addition to most of the favorite sections. And the content is presented in a number of different formats (multiple choice, matching, true/false, etc.) to provide a variety of learning methods as you go through. It is hoped that you will occasionally chuckle at what you find in addition to having a number of "aha" moments throughout this book.

In fact, if you don't find yourself having fun as you go through this little book, you'd better double-check . . . you might be a Bible scholar.

**POCKET
BIBLE
TRIVIA**

1

Identify the Quote

The Bible is the source of many of our everyday quotes and references. For example, when you hear people speak of "the writing on the wall" or a "doubting Thomas," they are using biblical references (whether they know it or not).

Below are a number of familiar sayings. See if you can identify which ones come from the Bible and which have other sources. (And give yourself extra credit if you can identify those sources.) To maintain a similar cadence, the King James Version is used for the Bible verses below.

(1) "I am escaped with the skin of my teeth."

(2) "The quality of mercy is not strained, it droppeth as the gentle rain from heaven upon the place beneath: it is twice blessed; it blesseth him that gives and him that takes."

(3) "Can the Ethiopian change his skin, or the leopard his spots?"

(4) "Lord, what fools these mortals be!"

(5) "To everything there is a season, and a time to every purpose under the heaven."

(6) "God helps them that help themselves."

(7) "To err is human, to forgive divine."

(8) "It is more blessed to give than to receive."

(9) "Whatsoever ye would that men should do to you, do ye even so to them."

(10) "For fools rush in where angels fear to tread."

(11) "Pride goeth before destruction, and a haughty spirit before a fall."

(12) "Hope springs eternal in the human breast."

(13) "The love of money is the root of all evil."

(14) "Train up a child in the way he should go: and when he is old, he will not depart from it."

(15) "Spare the rod, and spoil the child."

2

It's a Miracle!

When you think of miracles in the Bible, it's natural to think of Jesus right away. Yet a number of other people either initiated a miracle or participated in one. Some were instruments of God who brought about the miracle; others merely benefited from it. Try to match the following miracles with the people associated with them (listed at the end of the chapter).

Miraculous Event

(1) Interpreted another person's dream without even being told what the dream was.

(2) Sat on a hillside during a battle; as long as his hands were uplifted, the Israelites would win, but when he lowered his hands, they would lose. (He also parted the Red Sea, struck a rock and had water gush out, and did a lot of other miraculous stuff.)

(3) Was bitten by a deadly viper; when he didn't die, the people thought he must be a god.

(4) Thrown into a fiery furnace so hot it killed those tossing them in, yet he and his two friends came to no harm.

(5) Called down fire from heaven that consumed a drenched sacrifice, the altar, and even the stones and the soil.

(6) Exhausted after killing 1,000 Philistines with the jawbone of a donkey, he prayed and God created a spring of water right where he was.

(7) Used only 300 soldiers to defeat an enormous enemy army.

(8) Summoned thunder and rain during the dry season as a sign for the Israelites.

(9) Stood before Pharaoh as he (not Moses) changed his staff into a snake, turned the waters of the Nile River to blood, summoned frogs to cover the land, and initiated a plague of gnats.

(10) An angel escorted him out of a maximum-security prison without anyone noticing until long after he was outside.

(11) As a sign that God had answered someone's prayer, this prophet prayed that the shadow of the sun would reverse itself on ten steps of a stairway—and it did!

(12) Because his victorious army was about to see the enemy escape into darkness at the end of day, he commanded the sun to stand still; as a result, "the sun delayed going down about a full day."

(13) Performed many miracles during his life (making an iron axhead float, curing leprosy, bring-

ing a young man back from the dead, etc.); but even after death, when a fresh corpse happened to come into contact with his bones, the dead man came back to life.

(14) He and Peter were approached by a beggar who had been crippled from birth; instead of giving him money, they healed him.

Peformed the Miracle

(A) Aaron
(B) Daniel
(C) Elijah
(D) Elisha
(E) Gideon
(F) Isaiah
(G) John (the apostle)
(H) Joshua
(I) Meshach
(J) Moses
(K) Paul
(L) Peter
(M) Samson
(N) Samuel

Who Knows His Moses?

The story of the life of Moses fills four books of the Bible: Exodus, Leviticus, Numbers, and Deuteronomy. Below are twenty questions covering just a few of the events of Moses' life. See how much you know about this fascinating Old Testament figure.

(1) When the Moses story begins, the Israelites had been in Egypt for about:
(A) Four years
(B) Four decades
(C) Four centuries
(D) Forty days and forty nights

(2) Moses escaped early death due to clever parents, God's protection, and:
(A) Egyptians with bad aim
(B) Dumb luck
(C) An accounting error
(D) A thrilling escape on an "ark"

(3) After being fished out of the Nile, Moses had a pretty smooth life until:
(A) Egypt lost a big war
(B) A woman cut his hair
(C) A famine hit
(D) He killed a guy

(4) After fleeing to the wilderness, Moses acquired:
(A) Flocks and herds too numerous to count
(B) A wife, a kid or two, and a call from God
(C) A bad attitude
(D) BO like you wouldn't believe

(5) God spoke to Moses from a burning bush and told him to:
(A) Don't just stand there; get some water!
(B) Start working out because times were about to get tough
(C) Go tell Pharaoh he was going to lead the Israelites out of Egypt
(D) Lead the Israelites out of Egypt without Pharaoh finding out

(6) Which of the following was *not* a sign God gave Moses to use if needed?
(A) Producing frogs from nowhere
(B) Changing his staff to a snake and back
(C) Turning water to blood
(D) Giving himself leprosy

(7) After Moses' first request to leave, Pharaoh forced the Israelites to make bricks without:
(A) Limit
(B) Pay
(C) Straw
(D) Bathroom breaks

(8) So God sent a series of plagues. Which of the following are *all* among the ten plagues on Egypt?
(A) Nile turns to blood, body boils, rats
(B) Frogs, flies, the Mummy returns
(C) Darkness, hail, lesions on animals
(D) Gnats, locusts, anthrax

(9) Which of the following holidays was instituted during the Exodus?
(A) Yom Kippur
(B) Hanukkah
(C) Passover
(D) Kwanzaa

(10) Which of the following was *not* taken along in the exodus from Egypt?
(A) Six hundred thousand men plus women and kids
(B) Silver, gold, and Egyptian plunder
(C) A mummy
(D) Lots of freshly baked, high-rise bread

(11) How did the Israelites know where to go?
(A) God showed them continually, day and night
(B) Bright yellow Egyptian road signs marked the way

(C) They knew the general direction of the Promised Land and took as straight a path as possible
(D) God gave them clear instructions prior to leaving

(12) After Moses parted the Red Sea, the last words of the Egyptians are:
(A) "Nah! Those walls of water aren't going to fall on us!"
(B) "Let's get away from the Israelites! The LORD is fighting for them against Egypt."
(C) "Who fears the God of Israel?"
(D) "Onward for the glory of Pharaoh!"

(13) In the wilderness, God fed his people *manna,* which literally meant:
(A) "Heaven bread"
(B) "Honey dew"
(C) "Tastes great, less filling"
(D) "What *is* this stuff?"

(14) Which was *not* a way God (through Moses) provided water for the Israelites?
(A) Moses turned a pool of rancid water sweet by tossing in a piece of wood
(B) God led the Israelites to an oasis of twelve springs and seventy palm trees
(C) Moses hit a rock
(D) Moses spoke to a rock

(15) While Moses was receiving the Ten Commandments from God atop Mount Sinai, the people were:
(A) Supporting Moses with prayer and fasting
(B) Feasting and joyfully praising God
(C) Going about their daily business
(D) Building a new, more accessible god

(16) The gold for the golden calf came primarily from:
(A) Ore found near Sinai
(B) Egyptian tombs
(C) Earrings
(D) Peoples defeated during the Exodus

(17) Before entering the Promised Land, Moses sent in spies who returned with:
(A) Milk and honey
(B) Pomegranates, figs, and one monster cluster of grapes
(C) Livestock
(D) Giant grasshoppers

(18) Ten of the twelve spies recommended turning back due to the immense size of the inhabitants. The people rebelled and God had to intervene to prevent them from stoning the few remaining faithful people. But one thing God *didn't* do was:
(A) Suggest he kill them all and let Moses start over with a fresh bunch
(B) Sentence them to 40 additional years wandering the desert

(C) Exempt Joshua and Caleb (the only two faithful spies) from his sentence on Israel

(D) Strike the unfaithful spies with a plague

(19) Moses was allowed to look into the Promised Land but not set foot there because:

(A) He was disobedient and lacked trust in God

(B) He chose to stay on Sinai, in God's presence

(C) He was becoming old and weak

(D) He was voted out of the tribe

(20) Moses was more _____ than anyone else on the face of the earth.

(A) Righteous

(B) Faithful

(C) Humble

(D) Patient

4

Not a Handsome Fellow

The Bible contains some breathtakingly beautiful passages. Then again, in other places are descriptions of some not-so-lovely things. Match the rather pathetic description below, taken straight from the Bible, with the appropriate person (listed at the end of the chapter).

Biblical Description

(1) "He had often been chained hand and foot, but he tore the chains apart and broke the irons on his feet.... Night and day among the tombs and in the hills he would cry out and cut himself with stones."

(2) "A rawboned donkey lying down between two saddlebags."

(3) "Afflicted ... with painful sores from the soles of his feet to the top of his head. Then [he] took a piece of broken pottery and scraped himself with it as he sat among the ashes."

(4) "A beggar . . . covered with sores and long-ing to eat what fell from the rich man's table. Even the dogs came and licked his sores."

(5) "A huge man with six fingers on each hand and six toes on each foot—twenty-four in all."

(6) "Red, and his whole body was like a hairy garment."

(7) "He had no beauty or majesty to attract us to him, nothing in his appearance that we should desire him. He was despised and rejected by men, a man of sorrows, and familiar with suffering. Like one from whom men hide their faces he was de-spised, and we esteemed him not."

(8) "A wild donkey of a man; his hand will be against everyone and everyone's hand against him."

(9) "Like whitewashed tombs, which look beautiful on the outside but on the inside are full of dead men's bones and everything unclean."

(10) "He was driven away from people and ate grass like cattle. His body was drenched with the dew of heaven until his hair grew like the feathers of an eagle and his nails like the claws of a bird."

(11) "Under a curse and driven from the ground. . . . A restless wanderer on the earth."

(12) " 'By this time there is a bad odor, for he has been there four days.' . . . The dead man came out, his hands and feet wrapped with strips of linen, and a cloth around his face."

Character Described

(A) Cain
(B) Esau
(C) Ishmael
(D) Issachar (one of the twelve sons of Israel)
(E) Jesus (based on an Old Testament prophecy)
(F) Job
(G) Lazarus (a friend of Jesus)
(H) Lazarus (a figure in one of Jesus' parables)
(I) King Nebuchadnezzar of Babylon
(J) The Pharisees
(K) An unnamed man with an evil spirit
(L) An unnamed Philistine

5

We Three Kings

The combined kingdoms of Israel and Judah had only three kings before they split: Saul, David, and Solomon. Each of the three is remembered for both the good and the bad events of his life and kingdom. See if you can identify the correct king associated with each of the following clues:

(1) Committed murder to cover up an act of adultery

(2) Known as "a man after God's own heart"

(3) A head taller than any of the other Israelites

(4) Built and furnished a permanent, magnificent temple for God

(5) Almost had his son killed for eating a little honey during a battle

(6) Once offered 1,000 burnt offerings to God

(7) Had 700 wives and 300 concubines, which proved to be his downfall

(8) Experienced both the Spirit of God who allowed him to prophesy and an evil spirit sent from God to torment him

(9) Had a son known for courageous victories against the Philistines

(10) After committing a sin, witnessed an angel standing between heaven and earth, bringing a deadly plague

(11) Accumulated so much wealth that silver was as common in Jerusalem as stones

(12) A wife once scolded him for acting foolishly (he was dancing as worship while under-dressed), and she remained childless as a result

(13) Was looking for lost donkeys when he was anointed king

(14) Ordered that the child of a prostitute be cut in half, which resulted in much awe and admiration from the people

(15) Consulted a medium (witch) rather than God and committed suicide not long afterward

(16) Had one son who raped a half sister and another son who tried to overthrow the kingdom

(17) Could not keep warm when he got old, so a young virgin was hired to be his bed buddy

(18) People from all nations visited just to hear what he had to say

(19) The only one not credited with writing a psalm

(20) Used as a reference by Jesus in his Sermon on the Mount

6

Complete the Psalm

It's the hymnbook of Scripture, a prayer book, and the longest book in the Bible. Psalms is also quoted more in the New Testament than any other Old Testament book. The 150 psalms contain a wealth of literature that is both applicable and memorable. Below is a sampling of quotes from the Psalms. See how well you do at choosing the correct option to complete each thought. But a word of warning: the various psalmists were very honest about their feelings. As you check your answers, you may be surprised at some of the things that are actually stated in the Bible.

(1) Blessed is the man who does not walk:
(A) Where his feet should not tread
(B) In the counsel of the wicked or stand in the way of sinners
(C) Away from the Lord
(D) Around in the temple when he should sit quietly

(2) O LORD, how many are my foes! How many rise up against me! . . . Arise, O LORD! Deliver me, O my God!:
(A) Provide your protection from all my enemies
(B) Forgive my enemies for their offenses against me
(C) Strike all my enemies on the jaw; break the teeth of the wicked
(D) Give unto me a life of peace and prosperity

(3) O LORD, do not rebuke me in your anger or discipline me in your wrath. . . . I am worn out from groaning:
(A) All night long I flood my bed with weeping and drench my couch with tears
(B) Yet I groan no longer for you are with me
(C) But you do not bless groaning, so I laugh instead
(D) And when you groan, the whole world groans with you

(4) Arise, O LORD, let not man triumph; let the nations be judged in your presence:
(A) Let your loving mercy shine on them
(B) Declare them "Not guilty by reason of insanity"
(C) Judge them with complete fairness
(D) Strike them with terror, O LORD; let the nations know they are but men

(5) The LORD examines the righteous, but the wicked and those who love violence his soul hates. On the wicked he will:
(A) Rain fiery coals and burning sulfur
(B) Rain frogs, lice, and plagues aplenty
(C) Reign in power and majesty
(D) Rein in their evil outreach

(6) How long, O LORD?
(A) How long is a cubit?
(B) How long may I continue to serve in your holy temple?
(C) How long must I endure the slings and arrows of outrageous fortune?
(D) Will you forget me forever? How long will you hide your face from me?

(7) The fool says in his heart:
(A) "Two plus two is five."
(B) "God will love me no matter how I behave."
(C) "I am in control of my life."
(D) "There is no God."

(8) The earth trembled and quaked, and the foundations of the mountains shook; they trembled because [God] was:
(A) Almighty
(B) Absent
(C) Angry
(D) Active

(9) May the words of my mouth and the meditation of my heart:
(A) Stave off the forces of evil
(B) Be pleasing in your sight, O LORD, my Rock and my Redeemer
(C) Keep me from getting into trouble
(D) Remain as pure as the newly fallen snow

(10) Even though I walk through the valley of the shadow of death, I will fear no evil, for:

(A) You are with me; your rod and your staff, they comfort me.

(B) Your power goes before me and your love follows wherever I go.

(C) Whatever happens, I am yours.

(D) I am the biggest, meanest son of a gun in the valley.

(11) Who may ascend the hill of the LORD? Who may stand in his holy place?

(A) He who has clean hands and a pure heart

(B) He whose great deeds are known throughout the land

(C) He who is strong in faith and steadfast in good character

(D) He who asks nicely

(12) My guilt has overwhelmed me like a burden too heavy to bear:

(A) Behold! It squasheth me like a bug

(B) Draw near and lighten the load I carry

(C) Remove this weight and I will serve you forever

(D) My wounds fester and are loathsome because of my sinful folly

(13) God is our refuge and strength:

(A) Who guides us safely through the wilderness

(B) An ever-present help in trouble

(C) Whose mighty works are known to the ends of the earth

(D) Who never turns his back on those he has chosen

(14) Surely God is good to Israel, to those who are pure in heart. But as for me, my feet had almost slipped; I had nearly lost my foothold. For I envied:

(A) My neighbor's shiny new chariot with its new-chariot smell

(B) The strength and power of the nations around me

(C) The arrogant when I saw the prosperity of the wicked

(D) The righteousness of the patriarchs of old

(15) O Lᴏʀᴅ God Almighty, how long will your anger smolder against the prayers of your people?

(A) We beseech you seeking compassion and forgiveness

(B) Without your loving mercy, we fall faint and never arise

(C) The loss of your presence is too much to bear

(D) You have fed them with the bread of tears; you have made them drink tears by the bowlful

(16) I would rather be a _____ in the house of my God than dwell in the tents of the wicked.
(A) Scorekeeper
(B) Doorkeeper
(C) Floor sweeper
(D) Bookkeeper

(17) The length of our days is seventy years—or eighty, if we have the strength:
(A) And beyond that, eternity with you
(B) Yet our years are but sand through your hands, O LORD
(C) May our lives honor you from cradle to grave
(D) Yet their span is but trouble and sorrow, for they quickly pass, and we fly away

(18) Unless the LORD builds the house:
(A) Its builders labor in vain
(B) It will never withstand the storm
(C) His people continue to wander as sheep without a shepherd
(D) It will never pass inspection

(19) By the rivers of Babylon we sat and wept when we remembered Zion. There on the poplars we hung our:
(A) Hammocks and lived in misery for seventy years
(B) Tools, determined to do no work for our enemies
(C) Harps, for there our captors asked us for songs
(D) Heads and prayed that God would soon return us to our homeland

(20) Search me, O God, and know my heart; test me and know my anxious thoughts.

(A) Forgive the iniquity you find in my life

(B) See if there is any offensive way in me, and lead me in the way everlasting

(C) Judge me not, for I am weak and weary

(D) Grant me your everlasting peace and help me live for you

7

May I Have Your Attention, Please?

As you read through the Bible, you find many different ways that God made his presence known. Some of the methods were unique, onetime phenomena. Others, such as dreams and angels, were used numerous times with various people, although only one instance has been selected for the purposes of this exercise. Match each person (or group of persons) listed below with the innovative way God communicated to either inform or confirm what he wanted the appropriate person to do. (Note: You may find more than one correct answer for a few of the methods listed.)

God's Method of Communication

(1) A talking (and quite intelligent) donkey

(2) A bush on fire that did not burn up

(3) People suddenly started speaking in different languages and couldn't communicate with anyone else

(4) People suddenly started speaking in different languages and could communicate with *everyone* else

(5) Loss of the ability to speak

(6) A voice in the night (four times)

(7) A gentle whisper (following a great wind, an earthquake, and a fire)

(8) Use of the Urim and Thummim (two sacred lots, perhaps stones, that were located on the breast-plate of the high priest)

(9) Casting lots

(10) A pillar of cloud and a pillar of fire

(11) Writing on a wall

(12) A blinding light and voice on the road to Damascus

(13) Angels who literally dragged people out of a dangerous situation

(14) A wet fleece on dry ground, and then a dry fleece atop wet, dewy ground

(15) Sound effects (the sound of marching in the tops of the trees)

(16) A dream of angels ascending and descending a staircase (ladder)

(17) A visit in a fiery furnace

(18) Overnight, the person's staff budded, blossomed, and produced almonds

(19) A prophet with a personal message (in this case, Elijah predicting a multiyear drought)

(20) The shadow of the sun reversed itself and moved backward along ten steps on a stairway

Communicator

(A) Aaron
(B) Ahab (a king of Israel)
(C) Balaam
(D) Belshazzar (a Babylonian king)
(E) David
(F) Disciples in the early church
(G) Elijah
(H) Gideon
(I) Hezekiah (a king of Judah)
(J) Israelites in the wilderness
(K) Jacob
(L) Joshua
(M) Lot and his family
(N) Moses
(O) Paul
(P) People building the Tower of Babel
(Q) Sailors on Jonah's getaway ship
(R) Samuel
(S) Shadrach, Meshach, and Abednego
(T) Zechariah (or Zacharias) (the father of John the Baptist)

8

Complete the Proverb

The book of Proverbs was written by a number of knowledgeable contributors, including Solomon, the wisest person who has ever lived. So here's a chance to see how wise *you* are. Below are the beginnings of twenty proverbs. See if you can choose the correct ending for each one.

(1) The fear of the LORD is:
(A) A path to righteousness
(B) The beginning of knowledge
(C) A result of the guilt of sinners
(D) Avoided by those who love him

(2) Trust in the LORD with all your heart and lean not on your own understanding; in all your ways acknowledge him, and:
(A) He will make your paths straight
(B) You will discover success and honor
(C) You will never find need to weep
(D) He will anoint you with power

(3) Can a man scoop fire into his lap without his clothes being burned? Can a man walk on hot coals without his feet being scorched? So is he who:
(A) Seeks dishonest gain, for he will never find contentment
(B) Allows his anger to get out of control; he knows not peace of mind
(C) Sleeps with another man's wife; no one who touches her will go unpunished
(D) Seeks wisdom through divination and occult practices; his future is ruin

(4) As vinegar to the teeth and smoke to the eyes, so is:
(A) The scent of an immoral woman
(B) The behavior of a rich and thoughtless man
(C) A sluggard to those who send him
(D) The advice of a fool

(5) Like a gold ring in a pig's snout is:
(A) A king with no respect for his people
(B) A judge who takes bribes
(C) He who thinks too highly of himself
(D) A beautiful woman who shows no discretion

(6) A wife of noble character is her husband's crown, but a disgraceful wife:
(A) Is his dunce cap
(B) Is like decay in his bones
(C) Must seek wisdom and honor
(D) Brings him only shame

(7) The way of a fool seems right to him, but a wise man:

(A) Isn't afraid to ask for directions

(B) Heeds only the Word of the LORD

(C) Listens to advice

(D) Is hard to find

(8) Diligent hands will rule, but:

(A) Idle hands are the devil's workshop

(B) Laziness ends in slave labor

(C) Sloth is a deadly sin

(D) All work and no play makes Solomon a dull boy

(9) He who spares the rod hates his son, but he who loves him:

(A) Needs not the rod at all

(B) Is quick to punish him

(C) Is careful to discipline him

(D) Picks up the rod and takes him fishing

(10) There is a way that seems right to a man, but:

(A) A woman quickly shows him why it is wrong

(B) He still loves to pursue folly

(C) It is the LORD's way that matters

(D) In the end it leads to death

(11) A heart at peace gives life to the body, but:

(A) Is as rare as a precious jewel

(B) Trouble is a snare that destroys contentment

(C) Men who rage against God are without hope

(D) Envy rots the bones

(12) A gentle answer turns away wrath, but:
(A) A harsh word stirs up anger
(B) A firm word is heard in the heat of an argument
(C) A kind word gains an even better response
(D) Sometimes the other person just needs a good kick in the seat of the pants

(13) Pride goes before destruction:
(A) As sloth goes before poverty
(B) And temptation goes before pride
(C) A haughty spirit before a fall
(D) The arrogant man will be laid low

(14) Better to meet a bear robbed of her cubs than:
(A) A woman scorned
(B) A fool in his folly
(C) A disobedient and rebellious child
(D) A used-cart salesman who won't take no for an answer

(15) Better to live on a corner of the roof than:
(A) In a home bought with dishonest gain
(B) In a field marked with the damages of war
(C) Work for an unrighteous master
(D) Share a house with a quarrelsome wife

(16) Train a child in the way he should go:
(A) And then you'll need to remind him a dozen times every day
(B) Yet he will seek his own path
(C) And when he is old he will not turn from it
(D) And do not despair when he strays from it

(17) An honest answer is:
(A) Likely to be rejected
(B) Like newfound treasure
(C) Like the brightest star in the canopy of the heavens
(D) Like a kiss on the lips

(18) If your enemy is hungry, give him food to eat; if he is thirsty, give him water to drink. In doing this, you will:
(A) Honor the LORD your God
(B) Help him see the error of his ways
(C) Henceforth have a friend
(D) Heap burning coals on his head

(19) If a man loudly blesses his neighbor early in the morning:
(A) It will be taken as a curse
(B) The glory of the LORD will fill the village
(C) He will prosper the whole day long
(D) His conscience is clear before God

(20) As iron sharpens iron:
(A) So one man sharpens another
(B) The soldier prepares for war
(C) The gleam of the metal is the pride of the blacksmith
(D) God's law sharpens the mind of a man

9

Dreams and Visions

In the Bible, God communicated to numerous people through dreams and visions: both believers and nonbelievers, in the Old Testament and New Testament. Below are just a few of the fascinating visions and dreams of Bible characters. Match the dream and/or vision with the appropriate person (listed at the end of the chapter).

Dream and/or Vision

(1) Dreamed of Jesus' innocence but was unable to sway a spouse who had the authority to prevent his crucifixion.

(2) Dreamed that the sun, moon, and eleven stars (representing his family) were bowing down to him.

(3) Had a vision of angels surrounding God's throne and was greatly upset at his "unclean" state until an angel touched his lips with a live coal.

(4) One of his five books of the Bible is almost entirely the account of a vision he had of the last days, including a beast (the antichrist), Armageddon, a scroll with seven seals, and the four horsemen of the Apocalypse.

(5) Dreamed of a stairway to heaven, with angels ascending and descending.

(6) Though his book is better known for other stories (such as a fiery furnace and lions' den), this prophet also recorded dreams and visions of assorted beasts, future kingdoms, seventy "sevens," God as the "Ancient of Days," and more.

(7) As confirmation that he would indeed have many descendants who would possess much land, this person had a conversation with God in a vision and saw a smoking firepot and torch pass between an array of recently slaughtered animals.

(8) Had a vision of a man begging, "Come over to Macedonia and help us."

(9) After being among the first to encounter Jesus, had a dream to return home a different way for safety's sake.

(10) Dreamed of three baskets of bread on his head being eaten by birds (which turned out to mean that he would die 3 days later):

(11) Had a vision of heavenly creatures moving on what appeared to be "made like a wheel intersecting a wheel"; the final nine chapters of his book describe his vision of a temple, those who serve in it, its furnishings, and its surroundings.

(12) Dreamed of a great statue with head of gold, chest and arms of silver, belly and thighs of bronze, legs of iron, and feet of iron mixed with baked clay; a rock struck and demolished the feet of the statue, then the rock became a mountain (a foretelling of the kingdom of God that would ultimately topple human kingdoms and last forever).

(13) Told by God in a dream to "ask for whatever you want me to give you" (he asked for wisdom).

(14) An angel warned him in a dream to flee to Egypt, which saved the life of the baby Jesus.

(15) Dreamed that seven ugly, skinny cows ate seven sleek, fat cows (signifying a coming famine).

(16) Had a vision where God told him to minister to Saul (Paul), even though at the time Paul had been trying to arrest all believers.

(17) After his first vision, this youngster had to tell his mentor some distressing news about the man's family.

(18) Had a vision of a large sheet lowered from heaven, containing both clean and unclean animals, and was instructed to "kill and eat." (The vision would later be understood as God's inclusion of Gentiles into the early church.)

Dreamer

(A) Abraham

(B) Ananias

(C) Daniel

(D) Ezekiel

(E) Isaiah

(F) Jacob

(G) John

(H) Joseph (the coat-of-many-colors guy from the Old Testament)

(I) Joseph (the husband of Mary in the New Testament)

(J) Nebuchadnezzar (king of Babylon)

(K) Paul

(L) Peter

(M) Pharaoh

(N) Pharaoh's baker

(O) Pilate's wife

(P) Samuel

(Q) Solomon

(R) Wise men (Magi)

10

The Writing Prophets

Many prophets are referenced in the Bible, but sixteen of them have books bearing their names. When we pick up the Bible for a little inspirational reading, many of us avoid the prophetic books—which comprise a hefty amount of the Old Testament. Yet you might know a little more about the four major (Isaiah, Jeremiah, Ezekiel, and Daniel) and twelve minor prophets than you realize. See how you do at matching the clues below with the prophets listed at the end of the chapter.

Distinctive Fact or Accomplishment

(1) Had much to say about "the day of the LORD" when God's judgment would be felt by sinful nations (he probably had to sit in the back at prophet school if they were seated alphabetically).

(2) Not only had a close encounter with some large felines, but also saw some incredible visions that figure into numerous interpretations of end-times events.

(3) Although the people of Nineveh repented after Jonah's visit, they soon reverted to wickedness and this prophet correctly predicted their eventual downfall.

(4) When the wise men stopped by Jerusalem seeking the Christ child, Herod's scholars consulted this prophet's writing to determine that the Messiah was to be born in Bethlehem.

(5) He is often referred to as "the weeping prophet" because he got little respect or positive response as he tried to prepare his people for a coming 70-year exile; among other things, his writings were burned, he was imprisoned, and he spent some time in a miry mud pit; he is also credited with writing the book of Lamentations.

(6) His eventual reconciliation with his promiscuous wife was a symbol of God's ongoing love and commitment even after Israel had deserted the Lord.

(7) "Will a man rob God?" this prophet asked his tightfisted people; he also predicted the coming of "the prophet Elijah before that great and dreadful day of the LORD comes," and he provided the final word of the Old Testament: "curse."

(8) This major prophet was more involved than most when it came to being a personal example of God's messages (for example, when his wife died, he was not allowed to mourn publicly because the temple was about to be destroyed and the exiled people would not be allowed to linger and grieve);

one of his best-known visions took place in a valley of dry bones and, according to an old spiritual, he "saw the wheel."

(9) He wrote the shortest of the Old Testament books of prophecy.

(10) He was a priest as well as a prophet, and his book records a number of spectacular visions, including a flying scroll, four chariots, and a woman in a basket; it concludes with the Lord standing on the Mount of Olives, splitting it in half.

(11) One of his prophecies was recalled immediately after the Holy Spirit first came to the believers of the early church.

(12) When the Jewish exiles were finally allowed to return from Babylon to their homeland, this prophet was there to exhort them to rebuild the temple that had been destroyed.

(13) This prophet, a shepherd and tender of sycamore fig trees who was called to prophesy to Israel, was a big proponent of social justice (he probably sat in the front at prophet school).

(14) This major prophet is mentioned by name twenty-two times in the New Testament—more than any other; one time in the synagogue at Nazareth, Jesus read from this guy's book and announced: "Today this scripture is fulfilled in your hearing."

(15) Unlike the other prophetic writings, this prophet's book is more like a question-and-answer conversation between himself and God.

(16) He resisted going to the capital of Assyria until a well-known incident with a fish; he later had a lesser-known encounter with a worm.

Prophet Described

(A) Isaiah
(B) Jeremiah
(C) Ezekiel
(D) Daniel
(E) Hosea
(F) Joel
(G) Amos
(H) Obadiah
(I) Jonah
(J) Micah
(K) Nahum
(L) Habakkuk
(M) Zephaniah
(N) Haggai
(O) Zechariah
(P) Malachi

Sixteen Horrible Deaths

We've all got to go sometime. [Actually, there are a couple of biblical exceptions: Enoch (Genesis 5:23–24; Hebrews 11:5) and Elijah (2 Kings 2:11–12). But most of us tend to die after we've lived our lives.] Still, some deaths stand out a bit more than others. See if you can match these graphic deaths with the biblical characters listed at the end of the chapter.

Circumstances of Death

(1) Head hammered to ground with a tent peg.

(2) The earth "opened its mouth" and they went down alive into the grave.

(3) The Lord's anger burned against him and he fell down dead after touching the ark of the covenant, even though he was trying to keep it from falling.

(4) Mauled by two bears after insulting the prophet Elisha.

(5) Had an assistant quickly kill him after a woman dropped a millstone from a tower and cracked his head.

(6) Ehud (a judge) plunged a sword into his belly and his belly fat closed over it.

(7) After being beheaded, the head was served on a platter at the request of an impressive dancer.

(8) Hanged on a gallows he built specifically to execute someone else.

(9) Thrown from a window by eunuchs and trampled underfoot by horses; by the time the dogs were finished with the body, all that was recovered were skull, feet, and hands.

(10) While hanging by hair from an oak tree, had three javelins plunged into heart and was finished off by ten soldiers.

(11) Butt of a spear was thrust into his stomach so hard it came out his back.

(12) Heard the ark of the covenant had been captured, fell backward off chair, broke neck, and died.

(13) Didn't correct crowd when they called him a god, so an angel of the Lord struck him down and he was eaten by worms.

(14) In spite of attempts to remain incognito during battle, was killed when "someone drew his bow at random" and the arrow hit him between the sections of his armor.

(15) Lied about a gift given to the church, and fell dead as a result.

(16) Either during or after hanging himself, "he fell headlong, his body burst open and all his intestines spilled out."

Victim

(A) Forty-two young men
(B) Abimelech (a rogue judge)
(C) Absalom (son of King David)
(D) Ahab
(E) Ananias and Sapphira
(F) Asahel (a brother of Joab, David's commander)
(G) Eglon (king of Moab)
(H) Eli (a priest)
(I) Haman
(J) King Herod
(K) Jezebel
(L) John the Baptist
(M) Judas Iscariot
(N) Korah and his followers
(O) Sisera (a cruel commander of an enemy army)
(P) Uzzah

The Original Christmas Story

Judging from lawn decorations in early December, some might assume that the first Christmas involved the baby Jesus in a manger surrounded by shepherds, wise men, little drummer boys, red-nosed reindeer, frosty snowmen, and numerous other characters. Yet of everything in the Bible, the one thing most of us know is the Christmas story . . . or do we? Answer the following questions and find out. You may be surprised how many—or how few—of our Christmas traditions are actually based on what's found in the Bible.

(1) The Jewish people were looking for the Messiah to come, but first they were to expect:
(A) A world of hurt because of their sins
(B) The prophet Elijah
(C) A great flock of angels with big news
(D) A sign among the heavens

(2) According to the prophet Micah, Jesus was to be born:
(A) In a miraculous way
(B) Out of wedlock

(C) In Bethlehem

(D) Under a bad sign

(3) The angel who told Mary to prepare for Jesus' birth was:

(A) Gabriel

(B) Michael

(C) John

(D) Denzel

(4) When Zechariah (the father of John the Baptist) questioned this same angel in the temple, God made him:

(A) Deaf

(B) Blind

(C) Dumb

(D) Lunch

(5) Zechariah doubted the angel's message that his wife, Elizabeth, would have a child because they both were:

(A) Sad and full of tears

(B) Scared and full of fears

(C) Young and full of beers

(D) Old and full of years

(6) When Mary discovered she was pregnant, she and Joseph were:

(A) Already married

(B) About to become engaged

(C) Pledged to be married

(D) Only hookin' up

(7) Joseph didn't take the news of Mary's pregnancy too well. He wanted to:

(A) Stone her

(B) Kill himself

(C) Publicly humiliate her

(D) Get a quickie divorce

(8) The baby was named Jesus ("the Lord saves") in response to whom/what?

(A) Gabriel

(B) Mary

(C) Joseph

(D) *1001 Hebrew Baby Names*

(9) Mary and Joseph were in Bethlehem rather than Nazareth because of:

(A) A famine

(B) Caesar Augustus

(C) A warning from an angel

(D) Some really, really bad directions

(10) Which of the following is the only correct statement based on the information provided in the Bible?

(A) Jesus was born in an inn

(B) Jesus was born in a stable

(C) Jesus was born among the sheep and cattle

(D) After Jesus was born, he was placed in a manger

(11) The shepherds first heard the news from:

(A) A single angel

(B) A multitude of the heavenly host

(C) The wise men
(D) Fellow shepherds

(12) The shepherds were told to look for what sign?
(A) A special star in the heavens
(B) A baby wrapped in cloths and lying in a manger
(C) A large gathering outside a stable
(D) A fish symbol on the back of a donkey

(13) Which of the following are the only persons you *will* find in the biblical story of the birth of Jesus?
(A) Three kings
(B) An innkeeper and his wife
(C) Terrified shepherds
(D) A choir of singing angels

(14) How did the wise men (Magi) find Jesus?
(A) They followed a star directly to where he was
(B) They followed a star to Jerusalem, where they received additional directions to Bethlehem
(C) They bumped into the shepherds, who pointed the way
(D) They were wise men—they just knew where to look

(15) When the wise men found Jesus, he was in a:
(A) Manger
(B) Stable
(C) Bassinet
(D) House

(16) The Bible tells of _____ wise men who presented _____ gifts to the baby Jesus.

(A) Three . . . three

(B) Three . . . an unspecified number of

(C) An unspecified number of . . . an unspecified number of

(D) An unspecified number of . . . three

(17) When the wise men didn't return to Herod as he had asked, Herod:

(A) Sent soldiers to retrieve them

(B) Went to look for Jesus himself

(C) Gave orders to kill all newborns

(D) Ordered that all male children under two be killed

(18) When Jesus was first presented in the temple, who recognized him as someone who would be very special?

(A) A man waiting to see the Christ before he died and a very old widow

(B) A little child

(C) The high priest

(D) A number of religious leaders

(19) Before Mary, Joseph, and Jesus returned home, they had to:

(A) Ensure that the wise men had arrived home safely

(B) Flee for their lives and hang out in another country for a while

(C) Baptize Jesus

(D) Register Jesus in the census

(20) How did Mary respond to all of the events of Jesus' birth?

(A) She was "sore afraid"

(B) She asked God a lot of questions

(C) She "treasured up all these things and pondered them in her heart"

(D) She sent clever, informative Christmas letters out to all her friends

13

The Life of Jesus

No short book can adequately cover the life and ministry of Jesus. But the following true/false quiz provides a brief sampling of the content of the Gospels: Matthew, Mark, Luke, and John.

(1) Even when Jesus was 12 years old, everyone who heard him discussing spiritual matters with religious leaders was amazed at his understanding and answers.

(2) Jesus was about 25 when he began his ministry.

(3) When Jesus was baptized by John the Baptist, he heard the voice of God from heaven and the Holy Spirit descended like a dove and rested on him.

(4) When Jesus was tempted in the wilderness, he had just fasted for 40 days and 40 nights.

(5) Jesus withstood each of three temptations simply by quoting a verse from the Scriptures (what we know as the Old Testament).

(6) When Jesus called Andrew and Peter to be his disciples, they were fishing in the Dead Sea.

(7) Jesus spent an entire night in prayer just prior to choosing the twelve apostles.

(8) One time Jesus picked up a stick and started driving animals and money changers out of the temple.

(9) Jesus raised three people (that we know of) from the dead.

(10) When Jesus said, "I have not found anyone in Israel with such great faith," he was talking about a Roman centurion.

(11) Jesus not only walked on water, but he also calmed a terrible storm just by speaking to it.

(12) After designating twelve apostles, Jesus later sent out seventy-two disciples in pairs into towns he planned to visit.

(13) Although most of the religious leaders opposed Jesus, a Pharisee named Zacchaeus met with him at night to discuss spiritual things.

(14) At a well, Jesus had an interesting discussion with a Samaritan woman who had had five husbands and was currently living with yet another guy.

(15) Although Jesus met with opposition in a lot of places, he was warmly received in his hometown of Nazareth.

(16) Jesus lived in Nazareth his entire adult life.

(17) It is safe to presume that Peter was married because Jesus healed his mother-in-law.

(18) Jesus nicknamed James and John (the sons of Zebedee) "Boanerges," which meant "sons of lightning."

(19) Jesus was known as a glutton and a drunkard as well as a friend of tax collectors and sinners.

(20) The ministry of Jesus and the disciples was supported financially by a group of women who had been cured of evil spirits and diseases.

(21) One time Jesus cast out a number of demons from a man, and they immediately inhabited a herd of about 2,000 sheep that then ran down a hill into a lake and drowned.

(22) A woman was healed of a bleeding disease that had lasted 12 years just by touching the edge of Jesus' cloak.

(23) One time Jesus fed a crowd of 5,000 men (plus women and children) using only five loaves of bread and two fish; later he performed a similar feat for a crowd of 4,000 men (plus women and children).

(24) Once when a non-Jewish woman asked Jesus to heal her daughter, Jesus told the woman: "I was sent only to the lost sheep of Israel. . . . It is not right to take the children's bread and toss it to their dogs."

(25) Three of Jesus' disciples witnessed his transfiguration when his face shone like the sun, his clothes became as white as a flash of light, and he conversed with Moses and Elijah.

(26) After Jesus raised Lazarus from the dead, the religious leaders not only wanted to kill Jesus, but they plotted to kill Lazarus as well.

(27) One time Jesus healed ten lepers and expressed disappointment when only half of them came back to thank him.

(28) At times Jesus had to break up arguments among the disciples about which of them was the greatest and even had to deal with the mother of a couple of them who requested special favor for her sons.

(29) One time Jesus cursed an olive tree because it wasn't bearing fruit, and by the next day it had withered and died.

(30) At the Last Supper, Jesus washed all the disciples' feet, although Judas resisted.

14

The Teachings of Jesus

The Bible tells us that when Jesus spoke, "the crowds were amazed ... because he taught as one who had authority, and not as their teachers of the law" (Matthew 7:28–29). Below are a few statements concerning his teachings. See if you can identify which ones are true and which ones aren't entirely correct.

(1) When Jesus started preaching, he echoed the message of John the Baptist: "Repent, for the kingdom of heaven is near."

(2) In the Beatitudes (the prelude to the Sermon on the Mount), Jesus said the meek were "blessed" because someday they would see justice done.

(3) Jesus said his followers could not enter the kingdom of heaven unless their righteousness exceeded that of the teachers of the law and the Pharisees.

(4) In the Sermon on the Mount, Jesus compared his followers to salt, light, and a city on a hill.

(5) Jesus said he had come to do away with the outdated Law and (writings of) the Prophets.

(6) In matters such as murder, adultery, and divorce, Jesus promoted narrower, more restrictive guidelines than what were being taught at the time.

(7) The Lord's Prayer is included in Jesus' Sermon on the Mount.

(8) The Golden Rule ("Do to others what you would have them do to you") is part of Jesus' Sermon on the Mount.

(9) Jesus told parables to clarify the mystery of the kingdom of God for everyone.

(10) Jesus reminded his listeners that the gate to heaven is wide and easy to find.

(11) Jesus told about forty parables, including one praising a dishonest business manager and one comparing God to an unjust judge who granted a request just to get a persistent widow off his back.

(12) Jesus lost a lot of followers when he started talking about people "eat[ing] my flesh and drink[ing] my blood."

(13) Jesus taught that the greatest in the kingdom of heaven would be those people who worked hard and remained most faithful to God.

(14) Jesus' parable of the Good Samaritan was preceded by a question ("And who is my neighbor?") and concluded with a challenge: "Go and do likewise."

(15) Jesus taught that considering becoming one of his disciples required planning and forethought in much the same way that a building project or military campaign would.

(16) Jesus' parable of the prodigal son concludes with a joyful reunion of the father and his two sons.

(17) Jesus taught that if the Law and Prophets weren't enough to persuade a person to repent, he or she wouldn't be convinced even if someone were to come back from the dead with a personal message.

(18) Jesus said that the entire Old Testament (the Law and the Prophets) was summed up in two commandments: "Love the Lord your God with all your heart and with all your soul and with all your mind and with all your strength," and "Love your neighbor as yourself."

(19) Jesus promised to return to earth after his death but said that only a few people would be able to discern the day and the hour of his return.

(20) Jesus told his disciples that anyone who had seen him had seen God the Father.

15

Jesus' Death and Resurrection

With the Gospels' four different eyewitness accounts of Jesus' death, we have a wealth of information to draw from. Some writers recorded certain facts, and other writers focused on different things. But they all agree that while the death of Jesus was horrid and brutal, his resurrection was glorious and certain. The following questions cover just a few of the events of the last days of Jesus on earth.

(1) Which Old Testament prophet foretold a Messiah who would be "pierced for our transgressions," "led like a lamb to the slaughter," "assigned a grave with the wicked," and would "[pour] out his life unto death, and [be] numbered with the transgressors"?
(A) Isaiah
(B) Jeremiah
(C) Ezekiel
(D) Obadiah

(2) Many of the religious leaders had long wanted to silence Jesus, but they were afraid to do it during Passover because:

(A) It would have interfered with their family seders

(B) It was against their law to hold an execution during a religious holiday

(C) They were afraid the people might riot if they tried to harm Jesus

(D) They wanted his death to look like an accident

(3) Where did Jesus and the disciples eat the Last Supper?

(A) In the banquet hall of an inn

(B) At the temple

(C) At the home of Mary Magdalene

(D) In the upper room of a stranger's house

(4) At his Last Supper, Jesus identified Judas Iscariot as the one who would betray him by:

(A) Handing him a piece of bread

(B) Proclaiming, "You are the man!"

(C) Kissing him

(D) Washing his feet

(5) After the Last Supper, Jesus took Peter, James, and John with him to pray in the Garden of Gethsemane, but they kept:

(A) Discussing the meal

(B) Wandering off

(C) Arguing among themselves

(D) Falling asleep

(6) When the religious leaders arrived with Judas, Judas kissed Jesus and said:
(A) "This is the man"
(B) "What I do, I do for your own good"
(C) "Greetings, Rabbi!"
(D) "Seize him!"

(7) Before the disciples all ran away and deserted Jesus, Peter first:
(A) Whipped out a sword and wounded one of those present
(B) Began to weep
(C) Expressed his great faith in Jesus
(D) Tried to reason with the religious leaders

(8) What was the official charge against Jesus?
(A) Healing on the Sabbath
(B) Blasphemy
(C) Heresy
(D) Idolatry

(9) During Jesus' various trials that evening, which of the following officials did he *not* appear before?
(A) Annas and Caiaphas (Jewish high priests)
(B) Pontius Pilate (the Roman procurator)
(C) Caesar Augustus (the Roman Emperor)
(D) Herod Antipas (the Roman-appointed ruler of Galilee)

(10) Less than a week before his crucifixion, Jesus had entered Jerusalem triumphantly, riding on a:
(A) Chariot
(B) White stallion
(C) Mule
(D) Donkey

(11) Pilate first attempted to appease the crowd without having to kill Jesus, but what finally changed his mind?
(A) Jesus insulted him
(B) The crowd threatened to claim he was disloyal to Caesar
(C) The crowd literally dragged Jesus away
(D) He had scheduled a meeting with Herod and had to make a quick decision

(12) What may have been one reason Pilate was reluctant to have Jesus put to death?
(A) His wife had had a dream of Jesus' innocence
(B) He had been impressed during a previous meeting with Jesus in the middle of the night
(C) Jesus had healed him
(D) Pilate and Jesus were distant relatives

(13) Jesus was flogged, stripped, mocked, dressed in a scarlet robe and "crown" of thorns, spat on, repeatedly beaten on the head with his "staff," then crucified between two:
(A) Religious zealots
(B) Murderers
(C) Robbers
(D) Soldiers who had deserted their posts

(14) Pilate had a sign placed on Jesus' cross that said, in three languages:
(A) "Jesus of Nazareth, the king of the Jews"
(B) "This man claimed to be the king of the Jews"
(C) "Behold what happens to enemies of Rome!"
(D) "I find no fault with this man"

(15) From the cross, Jesus spoke to:
(A) Simon Peter
(B) His mother, his Father, a new believer in him, and John
(C) Mary Magdalene
(D) The soldiers who were mocking him

(16) One of Jesus' statements from the cross was a portion of a:
(A) Psalm
(B) Proverb
(C) Lamentation
(D) Prayer of Moses

(17) Which of the following events did *not* take place immediately after Jesus died?
(A) The curtain in the temple was torn in two, from top to bottom
(B) The earth shook and rocks split
(C) Tombs came open and many dead people came back to life
(D) The criminals crucified on both sides of him repented

(18) Where was Jesus buried?
(A) In a "potter's field" (poor man's cemetery) pur-
chased with the money Judas had received to betray
him
(B) In a tomb intended for a family member
(C) In a tomb intended for one of the disciples
(D) In a tomb intended for a rich and prominent
Jewish religious leader

(19) The people who anointed Jesus' body were:
(A) Nicodemus and Joseph of Arimathea
(B) A group of women
(C) The disciples
(D) Unknown because the Bible doesn't say

**(20) Jesus was crucified at a place called Golgotha (or
Calvary), which means:**
(A) Execution Hill
(B) Place of the Skull
(C) Hill of Pain
(D) Beautiful Overlook

(21) Jesus' resurrection was first announced by:
(A) A thundering voice from heaven
(B) The disciples
(C) Two angels at the tomb
(D) The risen Jesus himself

(22) The first to hear of Jesus' resurrection were:
(A) Mary Magdalene and some other women
(B) The disciples

(C) The guards at the tomb

(D) A group of believers in an upper room

(23) The first person to encounter the risen Jesus was:

(A) Simon Peter

(B) Mary, Jesus' mother

(C) Mary Magdalene

(D) John

(24) What did Jesus do to prove he wasn't a ghost?

(A) He let the disciples examine his hands and feet, and he ate a piece of fish

(B) He opened a door and walked into the room

(C) He ate bread and drank wine

(D) He embraced each of the eleven disciples

(25) How much time passed between Jesus' resurrection and his ascension into heaven?

(A) Three days

(B) One week

(C) Two weeks

(D) Forty days

16

A Baker's Dozen of Disciples

The New Testament makes numerous references to Jesus' disciples (or apostles) as a group. But as individuals, some of them get considerably more coverage than the others. See if you can match the clues to the thirteen disciples (listed at the end of the chapter). Why thirteen? You'll find out as you start matching.

Clues

(1) Was willing to die with Jesus, yet didn't believe in the resurrection at first because he had been absent when Jesus appeared

(2) Walked on water, but three times denied knowing Jesus

(3) Initially a disciple of John the Baptist who left to follow Jesus and immediately recruited his brother, Simon (Peter)

(4) Along with his brother John, was given the name Boanerges ("sons of thunder") by Jesus and was the first of the twelve to be put to death

(5) Always referred to himself as "the disciple whom Jesus loved"

(6) Once asked Jesus to "show us the Father." Another time was responsible for helping some Gentiles who wanted to meet with Jesus (perhaps they asked him because of his Greek-sounding name)

(7) Though he was skeptical when told about Jesus, at their first meeting Jesus called him "a true Israelite, in whom there is nothing false"

(8) Was collecting taxes when Jesus called him

(9) His name is often followed by "the Little" or "the Younger" to differentiate him from another disciple with the same name

(10) He may have belonged to a radical political party opposed to Roman control of his country

(11) Nothing significant is known of him, but he is called Thaddaeus in a couple of places (and if you had his name today, you might prefer a different one as well)

(12) The treasurer for the disciples . . . and probably not a wise choice

(13) Chosen by casting lots to replace Judas Iscariot (after his suicide) as one of the apostles

Disciple Described

(A)   Andrew
(B)   James (son of Zebedee)
(C)   James (son of Alphaeus)
(D)   John
(E)   Judas Iscariot
(F)   Judas (son of James)
(G)   Matthew (Levi)
(H)   Matthias
(I)   Nathanael (Bartholomew)
(J)   Philip
(K)   Simon Peter
(L)   Simon the Zealot
(M)   Thomas

17

Sound Bytes

The Bible doesn't just tell stories. Many times it records the conversations and statements of its characters, not unlike the highlights of a nightly newscast. See if you can match each of the following sound bytes with the appropriate speaker (listed at the end of the chapter).

Biblical Quote

(1) "How will this be, since I am a virgin?"

(2) "Curse God and die!"

(3) "Listen, you rebels, must we bring you water out of this rock?"

(4) "Where you go I will go, and where you stay I will stay. Your people will be my people and your God my God."

(5) "You are the Christ, the Son of the living God."

(6) "And spare my people—this is my request. For I and my people have been sold for destruction and slaughter and annihilation."

(7) "Look, I see heaven open and the Son of Man standing at the right hand of God."

(8) "Among you stands one you do not know. He is the one who comes after me, the thongs of whose sandals I am not worthy to untie."

(9) "Jerusalem lies in ruins, and its gates have been burned with fire. Come, let us rebuild the wall of Jerusalem, and we will no longer be in disgrace."

(10) "Unless I see the nail marks in his hands and put my finger where the nails were, and put my hand into his side, I will not believe it."

(11) "I know that my Redeemer lives, and that in the end he will stand upon the earth."

(12) "Surely he was the Son of God!"

(13) "Choose for yourselves this day whom you will serve. . . . But as for me and my household, we will serve the LORD."

(14) "You are the man!"

(15) "You have been unfaithful; you have married foreign women. . . . Separate yourselves from the peoples around you and from your foreign wives."

(16) "Do you understand what you are reading?"

(17) "Look, Lord! Here and now I give half of my possessions to the poor, and if I have cheated anybody out of anything, I will pay back four times the amount."

(18) "Pick me up and throw me into the sea, and it will become calm."

(19) "My master has withheld nothing from me except you, because you are his wife. How then could I do such a wicked thing and sin against God?"

(20) "How can a man be born when he is old? Surely he cannot enter a second time into his mother's womb to be born!"

(21) "Here am I. Send me!"

(22) "The Lord who delivered me from the paw of the lion and the paw of the bear will deliver me from the hand of this Philistine."

(23) "Give me here on a platter the head of John the Baptist."

(24) "Shall I crucify your king?"

(25) "Please test your servants for ten days: Give us nothing but vegetables to eat and water to drink. Then compare our appearance with that of the young men who eat the royal food."

Speaker

(A) Centurion at Jesus' crucifixion
(B) Daniel
(C) Daughter of Herodias (probably Salome)
(D) David
(E) Esther
(F) Ezra
(G) Isaiah
(H) Job

(I)   Job's wife

(J)   John the Baptist

(K)   Jonah

(L)   Joseph (the one in the Old Testament)

(M)   Joshua

(N)   Mary

(O)   Moses

(P)   Nathan

(Q)   Nehemiah

(R)   Nicodemus

(S)   Philip (the deacon, not the apostle)

(T)   Pontius Pilate

(U)   Ruth

(V)   Simon Peter

(W)   Stephen (a leader of the early church)

(X)   Thomas

(Y)   Zacchaeus

18

The Life of Paul

Next to Jesus, Paul is probably the most prominent person in the New Testament. We discover much about his fascinating life in the last half of the book of Acts, and other helpful clues are found throughout his letters as well. See how much you know about Paul with the following exercise. Since it's in true-or-false format, you'll have a fifty-fifty chance of getting correct answers even on those you don't know!

(1) Paul was originally named Saul, but God changed his name to Paul.

(2) The first time we see Paul in the Bible, he is tending to the clothes of a crowd of men stoning a believer to death.

(3) Paul was born in Tarsus, a capital city known for its intellectual atmosphere and civic pride.

(4) Of the twenty-seven books in the New Testament, Paul is credited with writing thirteen of them.

(5) Paul was a Roman citizen.

(6) Paul received essentially all of his religious training after he had a dramatic conversion to Christianity.

(7) Paul's conversion took place while he was traveling from Damascus to Jerusalem.

(8) After Paul's initial encounter with Jesus, he was blind for 3 days.

(9) The believers were reluctant to trust Paul until God directed Peter to meet with him and welcome him into the church.

(10) Saul's conversion alarmed the Jewish religious leaders to the point that they staked out the city gates, planning to kill him, and Paul's new friends had to help him escape Damascus by lowering him down the wall in a basket.

(11) Paul went on a number of missionary journeys, telling people about Jesus and establishing churches, the first of which he traveled to with a faithful disciple named Barnabas and a young believer named John Mark.

(12) A disagreement between Paul and Barnabas prevented them from taking additional trips together.

(13) At one of their stops, Paul and his companion were mistaken for the Greek gods Zeus and Hermes, and the people brought animals to sacrifice to them.

(14) On Paul's first journey, he was stoned by a hostile crowd and left for dead.

(15) Paul had hoped to return from his first journey in time to attend a council in Jerusalem but missed it due to the events of his trip.

(16) On his second journey, Paul cast a spirit out of a pesky slave girl in Philippi, which led to his being arrested, stripped, flogged, and jailed.

(17) An angel miraculously helped Paul escape prison in the middle of the night.

(18) In Athens, Paul found a good opportunity to tell others about Jesus when he came upon an altar with the inscription: "To an Unknown God."

(19) Paul never stayed more than a few months in one place before moving on to another.

(20) In one place, God worked through Paul so that handkerchiefs he had touched could be carried to sick people who would then be healed or released from an evil spirit.

(21) Paul ran into trouble in Ephesus when a religious revival threatened the business of a craftsmen's guild that made their income selling silver shrines of the goddess Hera.

(22) One time a young man fell asleep during one of Paul's sermons and died from a fall from a third-story window ledge, but Paul brought him back to life.

(23) A prophet used Paul's belt to warn him that he would run into trouble if he went to Jerusalem, but Paul went anyway.

(24) One time Paul caused suspicion because he was mistaken for an Egyptian terrorist.

(25) More than forty men took a solemn oath not to eat or drink anything until they had killed Paul.

(26) None of Paul's trials took very long. Each time he was arrested, he was released in a matter of days.

(27) At one point Paul might have been released, but he demanded a trial before Caesar, which necessitated a trip to Rome.

(28) Paul was once involved in a devastating shipwreck, but thanks to him no one died.

(29) Paul was bitten by a deadly viper, and when he didn't die as a result, the witnesses assumed he was a god.

(30) The book of Acts has a happy ending, as Paul was declared not guilty and released to continue his ministry.

19

The Writings of Paul

When Paul wasn't on the road traveling, preaching, and establishing churches, he was frequently writing to comfort, advise, or encourage a person or church. Below are just a few of the things he wrote ... or then again, maybe he didn't. Can you tell Paul's genuine writings from the misstatements and inventions?

(1) In his writings, Paul occasionally expressed his own opinions along with inspired "comments from the Lord."

(2) Paul wrote that believers become not only God's children, but also his heirs—and coheirs with Jesus.

(3) In Paul's "love chapter" (1 Corinthians 13), he reminds us that knowledge, faith, and love will endure forever.

(4) Paul wrote of being imprisoned, flogged, beaten, stoned, shipwrecked (three times), adrift in the open sea for a night and a day, and numerous other sufferings.

(5) Paul calls his readers to be living sacrifices who conform to the world yet also are obedient to God.

(6) Paul described an "armor of God" for believers to wear that includes a belt of truth, shield of faith, and helmet of salvation, among other items.

(7) Paul referred to himself as the worst (or chief) of sinners.

(8) When Paul heard of a church member in a relationship with his father's wife (probably the man's stepmother), he advised that the church elders immediately meet with the man, pray with him, and restore him to fellowship.

(9) Paul tells believers to "pray continually."

(10) When Paul heard of two women involved in a public church disagreement, he called them by name in a letter, asking them to settle the matter.

(11) According to Paul, some people face temptations too powerful for anyone to endure, so other believers should remain alert and help see them through those situations.

(12) One time Paul wrote of a man who had been caught up into the seventh heaven where he heard inexpressible things he was not permitted to tell.

(13) Paul spoke in tongues.

(14) Paul assures us that we will have bodies in heaven, although they will be different from our earthly bodies.

(15) Paul compared the light of God in a believer's life to a treasure within a metal box.

(16) Paul says one good way to make sure others learn about Jesus is to become "yoked together" with unbelievers so that opportunities present themselves.

(17) Paul expressed a willingness to be cursed and cut off from Christ if it would somehow help his fellow Jews to believe in Jesus.

(18) Satan gave Paul a "thorn in [his] flesh" that God would not remove, even though Paul pleaded three times.

(19) Paul considered himself "crucified with Christ."

(20) Paul defined the "fruit of the Spirit" as "love, joy, peace, patience, kindness, goodness, faithfulness, gentleness and self-control."

(21) Paul tells believers that "each one should carry his own load" yet also acknowledges there are times when we should "carry each other's burdens."

(22) According to Paul, God's will is always going to be a mystery to us.

(23) When an outspoken group of agitators tried to demand circumcision for all believers, Paul wrote that he wished they would go the whole way and emasculate themselves.

(24) Paul said it's a good thing salvation comes by the grace of God because if it were based on good works, believers would tend to brag.

(25) Paul's letter to Philemon was primarily in regard to a runaway slave.

(26) Since God establishes all earthly authorities, Paul said, we are to submit to our governing bodies regardless of what we feel about them.

(27) Paul struggled to decide which he wanted more: to die or to continue to live.

(28) Paul said if unmarried people can't control themselves, it's better to marry than to burn with passion.

(29) Paul wrote Philippians, perhaps his most optimistic and joyful letter, while imprisoned.

(30) Paul recommended that when slaves became believers, their believing masters should set them free.

(31) Paul wrote that it is better to be wronged and cheated than for believers to file lawsuits against one another.

(32) Paul wrote that the anticipated return of Jesus is an event that should strike fear and terror in even the most faithful of believers.

(33) Paul says we should choose *not* to exercise certain spiritual freedoms in order to avoid creating a stumbling block for other believers who don't feel the same way.

(34) Paul assured Timothy, a young pastor, that the youngster's "spirit of timidity" was a gift from God.

(35) It is Paul's advice to make it a rule not to go to bed angry.

Where Do Babies Come From?

We may *think* we know where babies come from. But in the stories of the Bible, they come from letting husbands sleep with handmaids, from bartering for time with a mutual husband, from intense prayer, and from some far less noble methods. See what you know about the following biblical baby stories.

(1) After Cain killed Abel and was sentenced to wander the earth, leaving Eve without a child, she was "granted . . . another child in place of Abel" and named him:
(A) Enoch
(B) Seth
(C) Noah
(D) Howie

(2) When Sarah was unable to conceive and told Abraham to have a child with her handmaid, Hagar, what was the result?
(A) Hagar was also unable to have children
(B) They all lived together, happily ever after

(C) Hagar's baby created jealousy, and Sarah kicked them both out of the household

(D) Sarah became pregnant almost immediately

(3) After God told Rebekah, "Two nations are in your womb," what was unusual about the births of her twins, Jacob and Esau?

(A) They were conjoined

(B) They were identical, and no one could tell them apart

(C) The older one died almost immediately

(D) The younger one came out of the womb grasping the heel of the older one

(4) When Jacob's wives were competing to have children, what did Leah trade to her sister, Rachel, for the opportunity to sleep with their mutual husband?

(A) A new robe

(B) Mandrakes

(C) Five young lambs

(D) A time-share in the Dead Sea Saltwater Condominiums

(5) After Lot's daughters left Sodom and found themselves with no prospective husbands, they:

(A) Took vows of chastity

(B) Took turns getting their father drunk and sleeping with him

(C) Took their time until God provided them with husbands

(D) Took up occult practices in a desperate attempt to marry

(6) Prior to giving birth to Samuel, Hannah was childless and miserable, and she prayed so intently that a priest thought she was:

(A) Drunk

(B) Insane

(C) An angel

(D) Possessed

(7) What biblical figure was found as a baby and brought up as royalty, yet was also raised by his own mother?

(A) Saul

(B) David

(C) Solomon

(D) Moses

(8) The prophet Hosea had an unfaithful wife and children (perhaps not his) whose names meant:

(A) "New Hope" and "Perseverance"

(B) "Why, Lord?" and "Second Chance"

(C) "Not Loved" and "Not My People"

(D) "Get Lost" and "Don't Come Back"

(9) Onan was a guy who tried to avoid providing children for his sister-in-law by:

(A) Never sleeping with her

(B) Killing their children as soon as they were born

(C) Spilling his semen on the ground

(D) Constantly standing close to the microwave

(10) Samson's parents were unable to have children until an angel told them to await his birth. And after spending time with each of them, the angel:

(A) Warned them not to speak of what they had seen and heard

(B) Shone with the radiance of the sun

(C) Ascended to heaven in the flame of a sacrificed goat

(D) Heard a bell ring and got his wings

(11) The father of John the Baptist doubted the angel-delivered news that his elderly wife would soon bear a son, and as a result he was:

(A) Unable to speak until John was born

(B) Immediately put to death

(C) Blinded for the rest of his life

(D) Temporarily stricken with leprosy

(12) Mary was chosen to give birth to Jesus because:

(A) She had found favor with God

(B) She made offerings on a regular basis

(C) Her loyalty to Joseph was exemplary

(D) She was from the right family to fulfill Old Testament prophecy

The Bible or the Bard?

William Shakespeare lived from 1564 until 1616. The King James Bible was published in 1611. So the language is similar. See if you can tell which of the following quotes came from the King James Bible and which were from the pen of the Bard.

(1) "The devil can cite Scripture for his purpose."

(2) "Be sober, be vigilant; because your adversary the devil, as a roaring lion, walketh about, seeking whom he may devour."

(3) "This thy stature is like to a palm tree, and thy breasts to clusters of grapes. I said, I will go up to the palm tree, I will take hold of the boughs thereof."

(4) "Who hath woe? Who hath sorrow? Who hath contentions? Who hath babbling? Who hath wounds without cause? Who hath redness of eyes? They that tarry long at the wine; they that go to seek mixed

wine. Look not thou upon the wine when it is red, when it giveth its color in the cup, when it moveth itself aright. At the last it biteth like a serpent, and stingeth like an adder. Thine eyes shall behold strange women, and thine heart shall utter perverse things."

(5) "The venom clamors of a jealous woman poison more deadly than a mad dog's tooth."

(6) "God defend the right!"

(7) "His horns are like the horns of unicorns; with them he shall push the people together to the ends of the earth."

(8) "Truth hath a quiet breast."

(9) "Eat no onions nor garlic, for we are to utter sweet breath."

(10) "He hath a heart as sound as a bell, and his tongue is the clapper; for what his heart thinks his tongue speaks."

(11) "Though I look old, yet I am strong and lusty; for in my youth I never did apply hot and rebellious liquors in my blood."

(12) "For scarcely for a righteous man will one die; yet peradventure for a good man some would even dare to die."

(13) "Behold, I have made thy face strong against their faces, and thy forehead strong against their foreheads. Like an adamant harder than flint have I made thy forehead: fear them not, neither be dismayed at their looks, though they be a rebellious house."

(14) "I hate ingratitude more in a man than lying, vainness, babbling drunkenness, or any taint of vice whose strong corruption inhabits our frail blood."

(15) "And whatsoever mine eyes desired I kept not from them. I withheld not my heart from any joy. . . . Then I looked on all the works that my hands had wrought, and on the labour that I had laboured to do: and, behold, all was vanity and vexation of spirit, and there was no profit under the sun."

(16) "Hath my master sent me to thy master, and to thee, to speak these words? Hath he not sent me to the men who sit on the wall, that they may eat their own dung, and drink their own piss with you?"

Answer Key

(1) Bible: Job 19:20 KJV

(2) Shakespeare: *The Merchant of Venice,* act IV, scene i, line 184

(3) Bible: Jeremiah 13:23 KJV

(4) Shakespeare: *A Midsummer Night's Dream,* act III, scene ii, line115

(5) Bible: Ecclesiastes 3:1 KJV

(6) Benjamin Franklin (Borrowing from Aesop: "The gods help them that help themselves.")

(7) Alexander Pope (Borrowing from Plutarch: "For to err in opinion, though it be not the part of wise men, is at least human.")

(8) Bible: Acts 20:35 KJV (Paul quotes Jesus as saying this, but the quote is not included in any of the Gospels or elsewhere in the Bible.)

(9) Bible: Matthew 7:12 KJV

(10) Alexander Pope

(11) Bible: Proverbs 16:18 KJV

(12) Alexander Pope

(13) Bible: 1 Timothy 6:10 KJV

(14) Bible: Proverbs 22:6 KJV

(15) Samuel Butler (Although give yourself credit if you chose Bible. Butler's quote may be based on Proverbs 13:24: "He who spares the rod hates his son, but he who loves him is careful to discipline him.")

CHAPTER 2: IT'S A MIRACLE!

(1) B [Daniel 2]

(2) J [Exodus 14, 17]

(3) K [Acts 28:1–6]

(4) I [Daniel 3]

(5) C [1 Kings 18:20–40]

(6) M [Judges 15:15–19]

(7) E [Judges 7]

(8) N [1 Samuel 12:16–18]

(9) A [Exodus 7:10, 19–20; 8:5–6, 16–17]

(10) L [Acts 12:1–19]

(11) F [2 Kings 20:1–11]

(12) H [Joshua 10:9–14]

(13) D [2 Kings 4:8–6:7; 13:20–21]

(14) G [Acts 3:1–10]

CHAPTER 3: WHO KNOWS HIS MOSES?

(1) C [Exodus 12:40–41]

(2) D [Exodus 2:3—The word interpreted "basket" is the same in Hebrew as the one used for Noah's "ark."]

(3) D [Exodus 2:11–15]

(4) B [Exodus 2:21–22; 3:1–10; 18:2–4]

(5) C [Exodus 3:10]

(6) A [Exodus 4:1–9]

(7) C [Exodus 5:4–9]

(8) C [Exodus 7:14–11:10—The ten plagues were water turned to blood, frogs, gnats, flies, disease on livestock, boils, hail, locusts, darkness, and death of the firstborn.]

(9) C [Exodus 12:24–28]

(10) D [Exodus 12:17–20, 33–38; 13:19]

(11) A [Exodus 13:21–22]

(12) B [Exodus 14:25]

(13) D [Exodus 16:15, 31]

(14) D [Exodus 15:22–27; 17:1–7; Numbers 20:1–11]

(15) D [Exodus 32:1]

(16) C [Exodus 32:2–4]

(17) B [Numbers 13:23]

(18) C [Numbers 13–14]

(19) A [Numbers 20:12; Deuteronomy 32:48–52]

(20) C [Numbers 12:3]

CHAPTER 4: NOT A HANDSOME FELLOW

(1) K [Mark 5:4–5]

(2) D [Genesis 49:14]

(3) F [Job 2:7–8]

(4) H [Luke 16:20–21]

(5) L [2 Samuel 21:20]

(6) B [Genesis 25:25]

(7) E [Isaiah 53:2–3]

(8) C [Genesis 16:12]

(9) J [Matthew 23:27]

(10) I [Daniel 4:33]

(11) A [Genesis 4:11–12]

(12) G [John 11:39, 44]

CHAPTER 5: WE THREE KINGS

(1) David [2 Samuel 11]

(2) David [1 Samuel 13:13–14; 16: 7, 13]

(3) Saul [1 Samuel 9:2]

(4) Solomon [1 Kings 6–8]

(5) Saul [1 Samuel 14:24, 43–45]

(6) Solomon [1 Kings 3:4–5]

(7) Solomon [1 Kings 11:1–11]

(8) Saul [1 Samuel 10:9–11; 18:10–11]

(9) Saul [1 Samuel 14:1–14]

(10) David [1 Chronicles 21:16]

(11) Solomon [1 Kings 10:26–27]

(12) David [2 Samuel 6:16–23]

(13) Saul [1 Samuel 10:1–2]

(14) Solomon [1 Kings 3:16–28]

(15) Saul [1 Samuel 28:4–25; 31:1–6]

(16) David [2 Samuel 13:1–22; 15:10–14]

(17) David [1 Kings 1:1–4]

(18) Solomon [1 Kings 4:34]
(19) Saul [David is credited with almost half the Psalms, and Solomon with Psalms 72 and 127.]
(20) Solomon [Matthew 6:28–29]

CHAPTER 6: COMPLETE THE PSALM
(All Bible references are from the book of Psalms.)
(1) B [1:1]
(2) C [3:1, 7]
(3) A [6:1, 6]
(4) D [9:19–20]
(5) A [11:5–6]
(6) D [13:1]
(7) D [14:1]
(8) C [18:7]
(9) B [19:14]
(10) A [23:4]
(11) A [24:3–4]
(12) D [38:4–5]
(13) B [46:1]
(14) C [73:1–3]
(15) D [80:4–5]
(16) B [84:10]
(17) D [90:10]
(18) A [127:1]
(19) C [137:1–3]
(20) B [139:23–24]

CHAPTER 7: MAY I HAVE YOUR ATTENTION, PLEASE?
(1) C [Numbers 22:21–35]
(2) N [Exodus 3:1–6]
(3) P [Genesis 11:5–9]
(4) F [Acts 2:1–12]
(5) T [Luke 1:8–22, 57–64]

(6) R [1 Samuel 3:1–10]
(7) G [1 Kings 19:11–13]
(8) L [Numbers 27:18–23] or E [1 Samuel 23:9–12] or A [Exodus 28:29–30]
(9) Q [Jonah 1:7] or F [Acts 1:21–26]
(10) J [Exodus 13:21–22]
(11) D [Daniel 5:1–6, 25–28]
(12) O [Acts 9:1–4]
(13) M [Genesis 19:15–17]
(14) H [Judges 6:36–40]
(15) E [2 Samuel 5:23–25]
(16) K [Genesis 28:10–19]
(17) S [Daniel 3:19–30]
(18) A [Numbers 17]
(19) B [1 Kings 17:1; 18:1]
(20) I [2 Kings 20:1–11]

CHAPTER 8: COMPLETE THE PROVERB
(All Bible references are from the book of Proverbs.)
(1) B [1:7]
(2) A [3:5–6]
(3) C [6:27–29]
(4) C [10:26]
(5) D [11:22]
(6) B [12:4]
(7) C [12:15]
(8) B [12:24]
(9) C [13:24]
(10) D [14:12]
(11) D [14:30]
(12) A [15:1]
(13) C [16:18]
(14) B [17:12]
(15) D [21:9]
(16) C [22:6]

(17) D [24:26]
(18) D [25:21–22]
(19) A [27:14]
(20) A [27:17]

(13) G [Amos 7:14]
(14) A [Luke 4:14–21]
(15) L [Book of Habbakuk]
(16) I [Jonah 1; 4:5–11]

CHAPTER 9: DREAMS AND VISIONS

(1) O [Matthew 27:19–20]
(2) H [Genesis 37:5–11]
(3) E [Isaiah 6:1–8]
(4) G [Book of Revelation]
(5) F [Genesis 28:10–22]
(6) C [Daniel 7–12]
(7) A [Genesis 15]
(8) K [Acts 16:9–10]
(9) R [Matthew 2:7–12]
(10) N [Genesis 40:16–22]
(11) D [Ezekiel 1]
(12) J [Daniel 2]
(13) Q [1 Kings 3:4–15]
(14) I [Matthew 2:13–18]
(15) M [Genesis 41:1–40]
(16) B [Acts 9:10–19]
(17) P [1 Samuel 3:1–18]
(18) L [Acts 10:9–48]

CHAPTER 10: THE WRITING PROPHETS

(1) M [Zephaniah 1:7–18]
(2) D [Daniel 6–12]
(3) K [Nahum 3:18–19]
(4) J [Micah 5:2; Matthew 2:1–6]
(5) B [Jeremiah 29:10–11; 36–38]
(6) E [Hosea 3]
(7) P [Malachi 3:8; 4:6]
(8) C [Ezekiel 1:15–21; 24:15–27; 37:1–14]
(9) H [Book of Obadiah]
(10) O [Zechariah 5–6; 14:3–4]
(11) F [Joel 2:28–32; Acts 2:17–21]
(12) N [Haggai 1; Ezra 5:1]

CHAPTER 11: SIXTEEN HORRIBLE DEATHS

(1) O [Judges 4:21]
(2) N [Numbers 16:31–33]
(3) P [2 Samuel 6:6–7]
(4) A [2 Kings 2:23–24]
(5) B [Judges 9:52–54]
(6) G [Judges 3:21–22]
(7) L [Matthew 14:3–12]
(8) I [Esther 7:9]
(9) K [2 Kings 9:10, 30–35]
(10) C [2 Samuel 18:14–15]
(11) F [2 Samuel 2:23]
(12) H [1 Samuel 4:18]
(13) J [Acts 12:21–23]
(14) D [1 Kings 22:29–40]
(15) E [Acts 5:1–11]
(16) M [Acts 1:18]

CHAPTER 12: THE ORIGINAL CHRISTMAS STORY

(1) B [Malachi 4:5–6; Luke 1:13–17; Matthew 17:10–13]
(2) C [Micah 5:2]
(3) A [Luke 1:26–27]
(4) C [Luke 1:19–20]
(5) D [Luke 1:7]
(6) C [Luke 1:26–27]
(7) D [Matthew 1:18–19]
(8) A [Luke 1:26, 30–31; 2:21]
(9) B [Luke 2:1–5]
(10) D [Luke 2:7]
(11) A [Luke 2:8–14]
(12) B [Luke 2:12]

(13) C [Luke 2:8–14 (note that the passage never says the angel *sang*)]

(14) B [Matthew 2:1–11]

(15) D [Matthew 2:11]

(16) D [Matthew 2:11]

(17) D [Matthew 2:16–18]

(18) A [Luke 2:21–38]

(19) B [Matthew 2:13–15]

(20) C [Luke 2:19]

CHAPTER 13: THE LIFE OF JESUS

(1) T [Luke 2:41–52]

(2) F [Luke 3:23]

(3) T [Matthew 3:13–17]

(4) T [Matthew 4:1–2]

(5) T [Matthew 4:4, 7, 10]

(6) F [Matthew 4:18–20]

(7) T [Luke 6:12–16]

(8) F [John 2:13–16]

(9) T [Matthew 9:18–19, 23–26; Luke 7:11–17; John 11:1–44]

(10) T [Matthew 8:5–13]

(11) T [Matthew 14:22–33; 8:23–27]

(12) T [Luke 10:1–16]

(13) F [John 3:1–21]

(14) T [John 4:1–26 (especially vv. 17–18)]

(15) F [Luke 4:14–30]

(16) F [Matthew 4:13–16]

(17) T [Matthew 8:14–17]

(18) F [Mark 3:17]

(19) T [Matthew 11:19]

(20) T [Luke 8:1–3]

(21) F [Mark 5:1–20]

(22) T [Luke 8:41–48]

(23) T [Matthew 14:13–21; 15:29–38]

(24) T [Matthew 15:21–28]

(25) T [Matthew 17:1–8; Luke 9:28–36]

(26) T [John 11:53–54; 12:10–11]

(27) F [Luke 17:11–19]

(28) T [Mark 9:33–37; Matthew 20:20–28]

(29) F [Matthew 21:18–22]

(30) F [John 13:1–17]

CHAPTER 14: THE TEACHINGS OF JESUS

(1) T [Matthew 3:1–2; 4:17]

(2) F [Matthew 5:5]

(3) T [Matthew 5:20]

(4) T [Matthew 5:13–16]

(5) F [Matthew 5:17–18]

(6) T [Matthew 5:21–32]

(7) T [Matthew 6:9–13]

(8) T [Matthew 7:12]

(9) F [Mark 4:10–12]

(10) F [Matthew 7:13–14]

(11) T [Luke 16:1–8; 18:2–8]

(12) T [John 6:53–66]

(13) F [Matthew 18:1–5]

(14) T [Luke 10:25–37]

(15) T [Luke 14:25–35]

(16) F [Luke 15:11–32]

(17) T [Luke 16:19–31]

(18) T [Mark 12:28–31]

(19) F [Matthew 24:36–42]

(20) T [John 14:5–14]

CHAPTER 15: JESUS' DEATH AND RESURRECTION

(1) A [Isaiah 53:5,7,9,12]

(2) C [Matthew 26:1–5]

(3) D [Luke 22:7–13]

(4) A [John 13:21–30]

(5) D [Matthew 26:36–46]

(6) C [Matthew 26:49]

(7) A [John 18:4–11]

(8) B [Matthew 26:62–68]

(9) C [Matthew 26:57;
Luke 23:3–12; John 18:12–14]

(10) D [Matthew 21:1–11]

(11) B [John 19:12–16]

(12) A [Matthew 27:19]

(13) C [Matthew 27:38]

(14) A [John 19:19–22]

(15) B [Luke 23:34, 39–43, 46;
John 19:26–27]

(16) A [Matthew 27:46;
Psalm 22:1]

(17) D [Matthew 27:50–53]

(18) D [Matthew 27:57–60;
Mark 15:43]

(19) A [John 19:38–40]

(20) B [John 19:17]

(21) C [Luke 24:1–8]

(22) A [Luke 24:1–12]

(23) C [John 20:10–18]

(24) A [Luke 24:36–43]

(25) D [Acts 1:3]

**CHAPTER 16: A BAKER'S DOZEN OF
DISCIPLES**

(1) M [John 11:16; 20:24–28]

(2) K [Matthew 14:28–31;
26:69–75]

(3) A [John 1:35–42]

(4) B [Mark 3:17; Acts 12:1–2]

(5) D [John 13:22–23]

(6) J [John 12:20–22; 14:8–14]

(7) I [John 1:44–51]

(8) G [Matthew 9:9]

(9) C [Mark 3:16–19]

(10) L [Matthew 10:4]

(11) F [Mark 3:18; Luke 6:12–16]

(12) E [John 12:4–6; 13:29]

(13) H [Acts 1:21–26]

CHAPTER 17: SOUND BYTES

(1) N [Luke 1:34]

(2) I [Job 2:9]

(3) O [Numbers 20:10]

(4) U [Ruth 1:16]

(5) V [Matthew 16:16]

(6) E [Esther 7:3–4]

(7) W [Acts 7:56]

(8) J [John 1:26–27]

(9) Q [Nehemiah 2:17]

(10) X [John 20:25]

(11) H [Job 19:25]

(12) A [Matthew 27:54]

(13) M [Joshua 24:15]

(14) P [2 Samuel 12:7]

(15) F [Ezra 10:10–11]

(16) S [Acts 8:30]

(17) Y [Luke 19:8]

(18) K [Jonah 1:12]

(19) L [Genesis 39:9]

(20) R [John 3:4]

(21) G [Isaiah 6:8]

(22) D [1 Samuel 17:37]

(23) C [Matthew 14:8]

(24) T [John 19:15]

(25) B [Daniel 1:12–13]

CHAPTER 18: THE LIFE OF PAUL

(All Bible references are from the
book of Acts.)

(1) F [The reason for Paul's name
change from Saul is never
explained in the Bible. Many

think he simply adopted a more Greek-sounding name as he took his ministry to the Gentiles.]

(2) T [7:54–8:1]

(3) T [9:11; 21:39]

(4) T [Romans, 1 and 2 Corinthians, Galatians, Ephesians, Philippians, Colossians, 1 and 2 Thessalonians, 1 and 2 Timothy, Titus, and Philemon]

(5) T [22:27–29]

(6) F [22:3]

(7) F [9:1–3]

(8) T [9:8–9]

(9) F [9:10–19]

(10) T [9:23–25]

(11) T [12:25–13:5]

(12) T [15:36–40]

(13) T [14:11–13]

(14) T [14:19–20]

(15) F [15:1–12]

(16) F [16:16–24]

(17) F [16:25–34—It was Peter who escaped prison with an angel's help; Acts 12]

(18) T [17:22–23]

(19) F [18:11; 19:9–10]

(20) T [19:11–12]

(21) F [19:23–27]

(22) T [20:7–12]

(23) T [21:10–14]

(24) T [21:37–39]

(25) T [23:12–15]

(26) F [24:24–27]

(27) T [25:10–12; 26:32]

(28) T [27:27–44]

(29) T [28:1–6]

(30) F [28:16, 30–31]

CHAPTER 19: THE WRITINGS OF PAUL

(1) T [1 Corinthians 7:10–12, 25]

(2) T [Romans 8:15–17]

(3) F [1 Corinthians 13:8, 13]

(4) T [2 Corinthians 11:23–29]

(5) F [Romans 12:1–2]

(6) T [Ephesians 6:10–18]

(7) T [1 Timothy 1:15]

(8) F [1 Corinthians 5:1–5]

(9) T [1 Thessalonians 5:17]

(10) T [Philippians 4:2–3]

(11) F [1 Corinthians 10:12–13]

(12) F [2 Corinthians 12:2–4]

(13) T [1 Corinthians 14:18]

(14) T [1 Corinthians 15:35–44]

(15) F [2 Corinthians 4:6–7]

(16) F [2 Corinthians 6:14]

(17) T [Romans 9:1–5]

(18) T [2 Corinthians 12:7–10]

(19) T [Galatians 2:20]

(20) T [Galatians 5:22–23]

(21) T [Galatians 6:1–5]

(22) T [Ephesians 1:9–10]

(23) T [Galatians 5:12]

(24) T [Ephesians 2:8–9]

(25) T [Philemon vv. 10–16]

(26) T [Romans 13:1–7]

(27) T [Philippians 1:21–26]

(28) T [1 Corinthians 7:8–9]

(29) T [Philippians 1:13–14]

(30) F [Colossians 3:22–24]

(31) T [1 Corinthians 6:1–8]

(32) F [1 Thessalonians 5:1–11]

(33) T [1 Corinthians 8:9–13]

(34) F [2 Timothy 1:7]

(35) T [Ephesians 4:26–27]

CHAPTER 20: WHERE DO BABIES COME FROM?

(1) B [Genesis 4:25]

(2) C [Genesis 16; 21:8–21]

(3) D [Genesis 25:21–26]

(4) B [Genesis 30:14–16—The shape of mandrakes suggested a human's genital area and so were believed to aid in getting pregnant.]

(5) B [Genesis 19:30–38]

(6) A [1 Samuel 1:12–20]

(7) D [Exodus 2:1–10]

(8) C [Hosea 1:6–9]

(9) C [Genesis 38:8–10]

(10) C [Judges 13:19–21]

(11) A [Luke 1:5–22, 57–66]

(12) A [Luke 1:26–33]

CHAPTER 21: THE BIBLE OR THE BARD?

(1) Shakespeare: *The Merchant of Venice,* act I, scene iii, line 99

(2) Bible: 1 Peter 5:8 KJV

(3) Bible: Song of Songs 7:7–8 KJV

(4) Bible: Proverbs 23:29–33 KJV

(5) Shakespeare: *The Comedy of Errors,* act V, scene I, line 69

(6) Shakespeare: *King Henry the Sixth,* part II, act II, scene iii, line 55

(7) Bible: Deuteronomy 33:17 KJV

(8) Shakespeare: *King Richard the Second,* act I, scene iii, line 96

(9) Shakespeare: *A Midsummer Night's Dream,* act IV, scene ii, line 44

(10) Shakespeare: *Much Ado About Nothing,* act III, scene ii, line 12

(11) Shakespeare: *As You Like It,* act II, scene iii, line 47

(12) Bible: Romans 5:7 KJV

(13) Bible: Ezekiel 3:8–9

(14) Shakespeare: *Twelfth-Night,* act III, scene iv, line 390

(15) Bible: Ecclesiastes 2:10–11 KJV

(16) Bible: 2 Kings 18:27 KJV

About the Author

Stan Campbell is a writer with more than twenty years of experience in youth ministry and fifteen years in Christian publishing. He is the author of numerous books and curriculum products for both youth and adults. He and his wife, Kathy, live in the Nashville area.